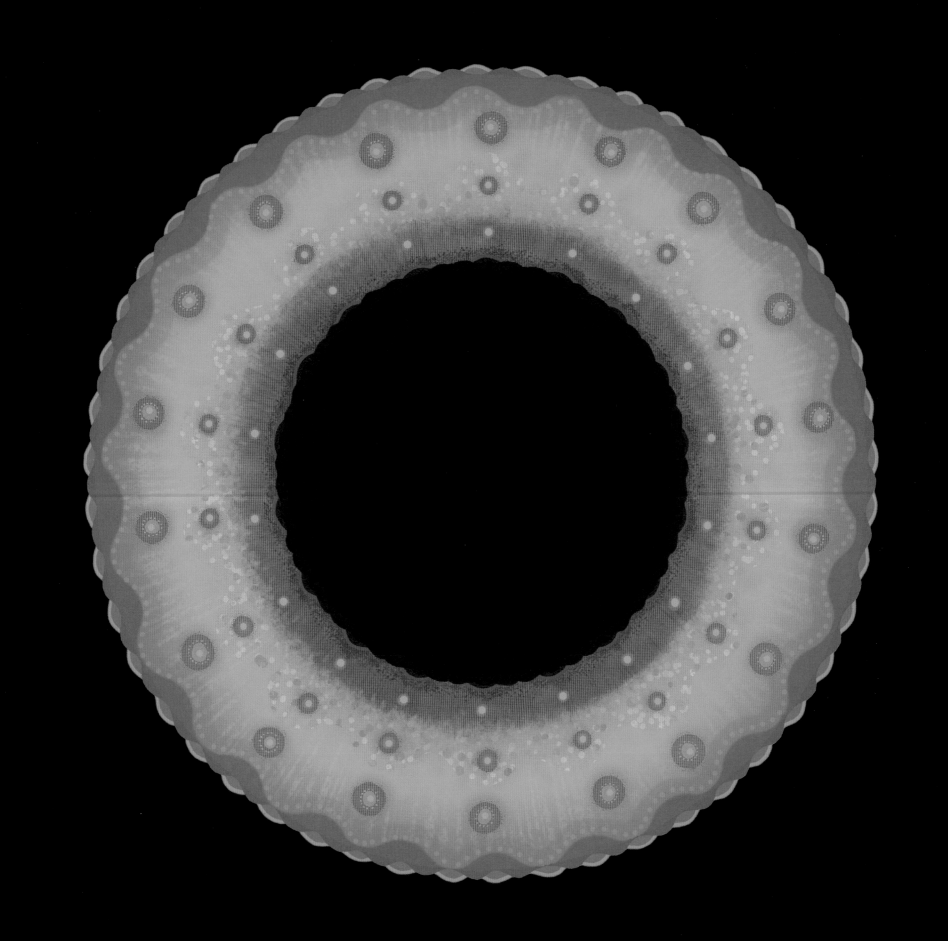

The Art of
DREAMWORKS
Ruby Gillman
TEENAGE
KRAKEN

Written and designed by Iain R. Morris
Foreword by Lana Condor

Cameron + Company
Petaluma, California

PAGE 1: YURIKO OTO • PAGES 2–3:
PIERRE-OLIVIER VINCENT • PAGES 4–5:
FREDERIC WILLIAM STEWART • 1, 3, 5–9:
PIERRE-OLIVIER VINCENT (AS RUBY GILL-
MAN) • 2, 4: FREDERIC WILLIAM STEWART

Contents

Foreword by Lana Condor ∾ 8

Introduction ∾ 10

Meet the Gillmans ∾ 19

Part 1: Land ∾ 43

Part 2: Sea ∾ 113

The Crew ∾ 172

Acknowledgments ∾ 174

Foreword

It has been a great honor and one of the biggest highlights of my career to be a part of *Ruby Gillman Teenage Kraken*. I play Ruby, an earnest, quirky, fast-talking, loving, nervous, big-hearted, friendship-forward teenager, who just happens to be a kraken. Oh, and let's not forget, an amazing mathlete!

Working with the incredible team at DreamWorks to bring this story to life was truly a dream collaboration. The kindness that I was shown every day at work and the passion each member of the team brought to the table to create the stunning world of Oceanside was unmatched. Every member of production put so much nuanced effort and focus into every detail of the story and animation—and shared the communal desire to transport our audience to a special, never-before-seen sea world. A world where anyone, or in the case of Ruby, a "normal teenager,"

can become and accomplish anything they put their hearts to. A world where being true to yourself is celebrated. A world where anyone can be brave, fight great battles, fully embrace what makes you unique, and flourish. A world where caring deeply for others is your biggest superpower.

As a coming-of-age story, showing the universal themes of teenage angst, the struggle to find yourself, the challenge of doing the right thing instead of the safe thing, and trusting in yourself is something that resonated with me, and I hope it does the same for our audience. Our multigenerational story, with Grandmamah, Agatha, and Ruby, also highlights the importance of family and shows that we are stronger together. Playing Ruby was a joy, and I, as well as every single person involved in the creative process, am deeply grateful and excited to share this fantastic adventure with the world!

Love, *Lana*

3

Introduction

IAIN R. MORRIS (IRM): What are some of the hurdles the producers and heads of departments had to overcome to bring the film *Ruby Gillman Teenage Kraken* to the screen?

KELLY COONEY CILELLA (KCC), Producer: This is one of our first wholly original movies in quite some time at DreamWorks Animation. It's not based on any existing intellectual property, so we're literally starting from the script that Chris Kuser had been developing. I immediately fell in love with Ruby and Agatha. I was excited about the tone of this movie in particular because having spent the early part of my career working on *Shrek* movies, I enjoy subversive movies about unlikely heroes. Ruby was an underdog to me because she didn't realize that she was special—that the thing that she was hiding from everybody was the thing that made her unique. When it came time to assemble the team, I knew we needed to have a strong, creative leadership team that could deliver the heart and the humor while also transporting us to an entirely unique new world.

We knew we had a great story with the script, but what we didn't know was, how are we going to visualize that epic kaiju battle? How do you do that in a way that still works with the tone of the comedy and doesn't feel like a separate movie? That has been the journey all along. Pierre-Olivier Vincent [POV] and Dave Walvoord, who had partnered on the *How to Train Your Dragon* movies, were great people to bring on board early, because they could really help us define the look. The other important person was Carlos Fernandez Puertolas, our head of character animation, who I'd worked with on *Trolls World Tour*. I knew he would completely be able to capture that charming, quirky character that Ruby was and come up with an animation style that fit the tone of the script. Then Jon Gutman, our head of layout, joined us, having worked on the last *Croods* movie—I knew that he also could do both. He knew how to sell a joke, but he also knew how to shoot an epic battle with larger-than-life characters. From the beginning, that was the goal: how could we form a creative leadership team with department heads that were the best in the business at what they do?

DAVE WALVOORD, VFX Supervisor: POV and I did *Dragon 2* and *Dragon 3* together, so we've got a great shorthand in our working relationship, but in a lot of ways, I end up off in my tech corner of the world, trying to figure out how to do all of POV's crazy designs! That's the fun and challenging thing about POV: he wants to show the audience something they've never seen before, and he really went for it in this movie.

CARLOS FERNANDEZ PUERTOLAS, Head of Character Animation: These animated movies are always tricky to make. The story that we started making early on is fairly different than what we're making now. I think our main character is the same, and the environment where the story happens is the same, but it's changed from what we started with. Early in the project, it was more trying to figure out the animation style, trying to figure out an anchor. For me, the anchor was being stuck in two worlds—Ruby, our protagonist, living with us, with humans, but being from a different world. Since we have two different worlds, we can play with the idea of contrast between the two. So I pitched the idea that the way we animate the characters that are underwater is different than the way we animate the characters that are humans. And for humans, we should play with the idea of being a little more solid in terms of the way we move them. By "solid," in animation terms, I'm talking about having very clear pivot points on elbows, with knees being a little more angular, and then the Gillmans will have a boneless feel to them—they don't have clear articulation points. They can do anything they want with their limbs.

JON GUTMAN, Head of Layout: When I came on, the pitch was exciting to me, and I loved all the artwork that we had seen very early on . . . the spirit of it has remained the same, but much of it has changed. There was a loose idea of a kaiju movie that meets a teen indie comedy, which I thought was interesting. And from a camera and cinematography standpoint, the merging of those two worlds seemed like a fun thing to do.

IRM: How did the look evolve?

KCC: Early on, POV had an idea about how you could take this world and make it not real-world but "real-world-adjacent." Everything has this very whimsical quality to it, where you feel like you could be in the Pacific Northwest or northern Europe, but you can't quite place what city you're in. And I think that was an important thing to establish from the beginning, because we're trying to create this contemporary-feeling world, with the way the high schoolers talk and behave, but at the same time, it's an imaginary, almost fairy-tale world. The Gillmans are blue. There's a big suspension of disbelief we're asking our audience to take.

PIERRE-OLIVIER VINCENT (POV), Production Designer: At DreamWorks, I don't think I ever had to deliver the entire look of a movie in less than a year—asset-created models and all that—and that's what we did. We did it at such a fast pace that everything was tight. For example, usually you would design, do a sketch for a design, then you would jump to a more finalized concept with the directors; then you do a page explaining the dimensions around that, and you give it to modeling. We never did that. We only did conceptual stuff, sometimes just sketches, and continued to final design through modeling and surfacing. We were involving surfacing and modeling at a much higher creative level than they usually are. They're very creative originally, but this time they were continuing the designs under my supervision.

IRM: In terms of a workflow, is this something that you think ought to be advocated?

POV: Double yes, triple yes, because by doing that, you train artists in other departments in the language of your movie. They're more involved; they're more excited by what they do, and you have an additional benefit of creativity every step of the way. And it's not like they can do whatever they want. I'm still there to just guide them to that vision that the studio accepted. But I think at the end of the day, you get much more. We were given a year to develop all that; we couldn't have done it any other way. I strongly believe that the art department wasn't separate; it was every department combined!

IRM: As a production designer, what else have you enjoyed, working within the parameters of your team?

POV: We have fantastic people in all departments, and I think because a lot of those guys I've known for years—Lawrence Lee, the head of effects; Dave Walvoord, the visual effects supervisor; Joanna Wu, head of lighting; and Jon Gutman, head of layout—we all worked together on the *How to Train Your Dragon* movies, so there are many shortcuts that you can use to get to the essentials right away. There's a lot of respect. One thing that I always loved at DreamWorks is the community we have. Some are just following you from movie to movie. Some are jumping on another

project, but they're always here. And I think it creates a wonderful artistic community. This has incredible value, especially when you're trying to do something different.

IRM: How did the characters take shape?

KCC: DreamWorks saw the potential in this film, but the thing that took us the longest to figure out was the character design, especially for Ruby, both for teenage Ruby and giant Ruby. What was hard is that she's a giant kraken, so by definition, she's a sea monster. So how do you make a monster feel feminine? When I finally saw this image of Giant Ruby, Giant Agatha, and Grandmamah in their poses, I was like, "Oh yeah, there it is." They feel strong and powerful, and yet still feminine. We probably had hundreds of different designs for what teenage Ruby would look like versus giant kraken Ruby, and it just really drove home for me how important character design is—it really becomes your springboard for everything.

I think that once we homed in on that round, tubular design language for Ruby, that then inspired the world for POV—it has lots of tubular designs so that she feels of that world, and then all the other characters also have that quality. And the big challenge here was, "How are we going to design a kraken that looks human enough to blend in with other humans, and how do you design the humans in a way that

BELOW: CONCEPT SURFACING PAINTING:
FREDERIC WILLIAM STEWART

they're going to be quirky enough that you believe she could blend in with them?" It was this real back-and-forth between those and trying to really get that character design right. We had several different character designers working with us early on as we explored the level of stylization and caricature that could work. Concept artist Timothy Lamb, who I worked with on the *Trolls* movies, had done some early designs when we were in development. POV came on board and saw those designs and said, "Well, why did you move away from that? That was gold. Let's go back to that." Timothy was no longer available, and so POV said, "Even though we don't have the perfect sketch of what this character is going to look like, let's move it into modeling so that we can explore her look in CG." That was one of the most exciting things about this movie for me. We didn't spend a lot of time on paintings and sketches. POV would build something rough, and then he would just pass it along and work interactively with all the artists. And I think it gave everyone in modeling and surfacing so much more creative freedom.

IRM: You've gathered your heads of departments; your supervisors as well. Where does your co-producer fit in?

KCC: Rachel Zusser has been my partner the whole way. She joined the team once the studio really started to put momentum behind it, and we started to build our green-light pitch deck with our budget and strategy. Rachel was crucial in the process of talking through how we were going to approach this movie: "What is the leadership we need; what's the makeup of the team?" We brought on Damon Crowe, head of character, and Jason Turner, head of location. Rachel was a big champion of them because she knew we had so much to get done in such a short amount of time. One of our biggest challenges on this movie has been effects, because our eyes have always been bigger than our stomachs! So we've had to really manage closely how we're approaching the effects, and what sequences they're in, and how much we see, and things like that. And Rachel, having worked with POV and Dave Walvoord on *How to Train Your Dragon 3*, knew them well and could help bolster that team. She'd also worked with Jon Gutman on *Croods*, so she knew our leadership team well and that helped in terms of the flow of communication between all of them and getting things up and running.

RACHEL ZUSSER, Co-Producer: When I first joined, it was interesting, because it was a film that had such great ambition, but it felt like it was a great idea with a story that just needed a little bit more finessing. Kelly basically hired me and asked if I wanted to go on an underwater aquatic sea adventure with her. That was probably the best way to describe what it was going to be and basically the best way to describe what we've been through.

IRM: How did the other departments fit in?

DAMON CROWE, Head of Characters: After they get past the artwork stage and flesh out an art model of the character, trying to figure out what it is in 3D, adding some rough textures on it, then I'll take it to the group. All the department heads and the visual effects advisors will start talking about how we're going to execute it. We have a lot of brainstorming sessions—a weekly character roundtable—where everybody would start breaking down the character. "Okay, Ruby's got hair that is kind of jellyfish-like, right? How gummy is it? How does it attach to her head?" We start breaking down the individual pieces for characters, and I'd speak with every

department that's going to work on her to make sure they're getting the right pieces at the right time. Animation has their own needs. In the rig, they'll say, "Well, she's going to have bendy limbs. We need to be able to stretch her arms. She's got suction cups on the pads of her hands that need to be able to key in and key out." So we'll start laying the groundwork for those pieces as we move forward. Then it just goes down the road. Then we're talking with surfacing, because inside these characters, we've got things that we didn't used to see. We have volumes floating around inside the characters, which is usually something reserved for the effects department to make. But we had to come up with ways to deform that via the rig and make it work.

MIKE MURRAY, Supervising Technical Director: Usually, as soon as we get into modeling or sometimes surfacing, we're going to have at least one technical director on to support these nascent departments early on. So, I did. I was the first one on, and then another TD came, and it grew from there. It was a wonderful environment of trust, and we all felt like everyone had plenty of experience on this movie. We felt that we were enabled to just move forward and move as quickly as we needed to with the schedule. But it's also very empowering when we're all working that way.

ABOVE: GUILLERMO CAREAGA

JASON TURNER, Head of Location: I've worked at the studio now for twenty years. I've worked on a lot of projects, and each one has its pros and cons. The most enjoyable part of these projects is the people. We're going to go through tough times, we're going to have budget constraints, but if you work with the right people, you can do a lot with less, and you make some concessions. But you also find creative solutions within a confined box . . . you have fewer pieces to work with, but you can put those pieces together in a creative way. You do have to push yourself to try to make it unique, but we have to all do it together. I really enjoyed the people that I worked with on *Ruby Gillman*. Really good group of people, talented artists.

IRM: At this stage, how has the script been coming along?

KCC: In the beginning, Pam Brady wrote several drafts. We were working really closely with Faryn Pearl, who's our co-director now and was our head of story at the time, developing this story. Faryn was one of the first people I thought of when I first came on the movie, because I knew that she would connect with this character and be the right fit for this film. When Kirk DeMicco came on board to direct, we had the opportunity to promote her because Kirk really wanted to have a co-director. I said, "Well, meet Faryn. I think you guys would really hit it off." And they did. They've got a nice symbiotic relationship. Kirk has been a great mentor to Faryn, this being her first time sitting in the director's chair, and he has so much experience; they've just been terrific partners.

Part of the script process is a lot of trial and error. When Kirk came on, he said, "I want to lean into the idea that this is a multigenerational female empowerment story. I want the story we're focusing on to be Ruby, her mom, and her grandmother. Everything else . . . let's strip it all away. How would we tell that story? And if those other things that we find really entertaining have a place here, we'll bring them back." We really stripped it back down to that core emotional story, and then over time, we started adding all the other elements back in. Kirk also championed another writer named Meghan Malloy, who worked with us and helped us through different drafts of the script. Then at a certain point, we were starting to put more sequences into production, and we just kept getting stuck in this one area, in the second half of the second act. In previous drafts, Ruby would go and visit her grandmother, she'd come back and be like, "No, I just want to go back to being a teenager." Then she would meet Chelsea, and they'd go on this girls' day out and have fun together as super sea-girl besties. But again, there was nothing really motivating that; they didn't have a clear goal that they were going toward, and so we came up with the Trident. How can we use the Trident—not just as a MacGuffin, but as an actual goal; if she can get that, then she will get what she wants.

To do that, we brought on Michael McCullers—who had worked on the *Boss Baby* movies, and who is an established writer, great comedically but also structurally. He came on to help us execute that idea and develop it further. We could use Gordon more as a misdirect for the audience so we could better hide that Chelsea is going to be the villain. You think Gordon's the one we should be worried about, because he's after Ruby, and this is just a girl who wants to be friends with her. He introduced the idea that Gordon tries to capture Ruby and that Chelsea saves Ruby, so it helps make it more believable that Ruby would trust her.

This movie has been such an education in terms of story math and puzzle-making because there have been so many different challenges that we've had to face—creatively and strategically.

IRM: Was the decision for taking on a co-director due to the time crunch and the need to divide and conquer?

KIRK DeMICCO (KD), Director: I had known Kelly Cooney Cilella from before, so I already knew our producer, and I had the chance to ask if Faryn could be a co-director on the movie. She was the head of story prior to me joining. She was somebody who was already on the team, but I had an opportunity to say, "Hey, do you want to do this with me?" It was really a great chance for me.

FARYN PEARL, Co-Director: I started this movie as a storyboard artist, so I only had such a narrow point of view at first, and now it feels like I get to see the whole movie for what it is. And I don't know if that makes me sound too green—and if it does, it's because I am. But it's been exciting to see animation, to really get to see the magic of that. Layout, I think, is a whole department that I did not realize how much pre-visualization really adds to the cinematography and tone of what we're trying to do.

1

KD: Faryn is very funny and brings a voice to the work. I love having that collaborative feeling to it. There's the work, but there's also the feeling of having two imaginations working together on one thing and then building a hivemind of talented co-workers. It's good to have people that I trust, and we all bounce things off each other.

IRM: What was your first task, then? You had a sort of rough script. You had the team in place, you had artwork; POV and his team were producing artwork. What were you then trying to accomplish?

KD: Trying to embrace the monster-movie part of the storytelling. We wanted to get into it fast—the idea of having her get in that water and have her first kraken experience in the first ten minutes. We brought the sequence where a giant kraken is discovered in the library into the first act and started working out the camera style with Jon. I wanted it to feel like, "Maybe it *is* scary." There's some in the beginning, so it takes you by surprise, for instance, when Ruby first goes in the water, and she's going to drown. It startles you. And then when she jumps across into that second act and into the ocean and to the kraken kingdom, it's a whole new experience.

IRM: Was there any artwork that had been done that resonated with you?

KD: The world of Oceanside with Ruby and her friends was set before I got here. And it's incredibly charming, whimsical. It was just really winning. It was a big reason why I fell in love with it. But the first thing was really storytelling and working with POV on the vision of what the giant krakens and their underwater world should look like. The giant krakens might have had preliminary sketches but nothing built, nothing really tied down.

Then we started to see things that POV and his team and Fred Stewart, his amazing art director, were putting together. They had done these beautiful images of the deep-sea canyons. There's no sunlight; there's nothing. And he had done these bioluminescence-filled currents, and it looked beautiful, like ribbon. It was so breathtaking that we were inspired to build what became the Well of Seas. That was a perfect example of what I love most about animation studios: things don't run one way; they go back and forth like that.

IRM: What has been the approach to the music for the film?

KCC: We really wanted it to feel like you were listening to the music that Ruby would be listening to. At one point she has her headphones on. "What is she listening to?" When she wakes up in the morning, her phone goes off, and a song starts playing. And as she's walking to school, there's another song playing. We worked closely with our music supervisor, Natalie Hayden at Universal, and she put together a playlist of songs, which she called her "teenage angst" playlist. We listened to it, and we thought, *Yes, this is it. This is the vibe.* We wanted it to feel youthful and fresh and current.

For the score, we really wanted to find someone who could blend the musical universe of the movie together, so that you didn't feel like one minute you were hearing Ruby's music, and then the next minute you were hearing a score. We didn't want them to compete; we needed them to blend. When we met with composer Stephanie Economou, she was like, "Underwater synth-pop!" Everything that she said, we were like, "Yes, that's the feel of it." The idea that the third-act battle would be played against a song, as opposed to score, totally felt like the right thing to do for us, because throughout the whole thing, we have to keep that youthful, playful, contemporary tone alive.

IRM: DreamWorks, I assume, has been supportive?

KCC: Yes, DreamWorks has always believed in this project. Margie and Kristin loved the idea that you're flipping on its head what you think you know about kraken versus mermaid. The mermaid is the mean girl of the sea, and she's the villain. I think they loved that idea. How exactly we would execute it was the challenge, especially finding the right tone. We knew it would be funny, but we also wanted it to be an action-packed hero's origin story, while also delivering the emotion, because at its core, it's a story about mothers and daughters.

2

1: Pierre-Olivier Vincent • 2: Timothy Lamb

Meet the Gillmans

ɔn the history of Oceanside, the Gillmans are unique. Sure, the town has visitors from all over the world (including Canada), but a family from the oceanic kraken kingdom? That's never happened. And to have that same family live and work there happily undetected? "Shrimpossible"! Yet this contented kraken family not only fit in—they also thrive. The paterfamilias, Arthur (voiced by Colman Domingo), runs his beloved antique shop; his wife, Agatha (voiced by Toni Collette), is a successful realtor; while the older daughter Ruby (voiced by Lana Condor) is in her senior year at high school. Sam (voiced by Blue Chapman), the younger brother, is at junior high, and the family pet, Nessie, is adorable if you like big-mouthed marine hybrids—and who doesn't?

The Gillmans are perfectly happy with life and, blue skin notwithstanding, are all settled at their various pursuits, as long as they follow the family rule: no going in the ocean. Never ever ever. Ruby, being a very honest and sincere girl, has obeyed this directive, but she's at the sandbar of teenage years and may yet run aground. Agatha is juggling a career, as well as a "fincreasingly" headstrong daughter and a secret from her past that threatens to muddy the still waters of family life as she knows it. It can't end well, can it? The Gillmans may feel like fish out of water sometimes, but as they always say, "When the going gets tough, the tough get kraken!"

"The easiest way to describe 'Gillmanizing' is really shape language, for modeling especially, and it doesn't always apply to characters. Say you're building a radio that's going to sit on the countertop. The Gillmans' version of that radio doesn't have any sharp edges; it's always rounded. It always feels like the aesthetic of this world, which has already been established by the buildings and everything else, but on characters you'll see all the Gillmans are softer and rounder than the humans. You start to get into our humans, and there's a little bit more detail for, say, a nose crease or something else. It's not as smoothed over, so there's a little bit of a distinction between the two."
—Damon Crowe, Head of Characters

"I think the comedy elements have to be part of the world-building. There's one very funny and important story element, which is the fact that our family of sea creatures are blue. They are blue, and they are living among the humans."
—Pierre Olivier Vincent, Production Designer

Ruby

Our heroine Ruby is made of the right stuff. No bones, but still, she's one tough jelly, baby! She's also a little lonely. Being blue, a kraken, and living a double life in Oceanside means she's never really felt she belongs. She has a few friends (her squad of other misfits), but she's still nervous around the popular kids, and as for asking her crush, Connor, on a date—she feels all adrift around him. In fact, life's not as swell as it could be. The prom is coming up, and it's being held on a boat. This is bad news, as she's not allowed in the ocean, and boats full of teenagers are notoriously unreliable out on open water. Of course, events conspire to have her dive headlong into the sea, where her latent kraken powers are activated. From then on, Ruby must deal with a new grandmother she's never met and the fact that her mother never even mentioned that Ruby was the heir to a kraken underwater kingdom. Plus, there's an old foe out for vengeance. Can mild-mannered Ruby embrace her inner kraken and take to ocean life like a duck to, well, you know . . . ? Wait and "sea"!

"Everyone connects with the idea of feeling different and feeling like they need to hide themselves to fit in and belong. I don't know a single person on this movie who hasn't said, 'Oh, I've been there; I've been Ruby.'"
—Faryn Pearl, Co-Director

1, 9, 10: Timothy Lamb • 2, 4–8: William Salazar • 3: Guillermo "Willie" Real

4 (INTROVERT — SHY?) LIDS DOWN

5 FLOATING MOUTH TRAVELLING MOUTH

7 THUNK

SORRY "LIQUIDY"

8 ALL THE WAY UP ONLY FOR UPSIDE DOWN POSE

"As a former teenage girl myself, I really enjoy Ruby's journey of going from a wallflower to becoming a warrior. And throughout the perils of adolescence and being a teenager, it's so refreshing to see a film of female empowerment, coming into your own, and really harnessing who you are on the inside for good."
—Rachel Zusser, Co-Producer

"Lana Condor has a deep, beautiful, natural connection to this story. She brings such warmth to Ruby, but at the same time, great comedic timing and has such a great delivery in making us feel the spontaneity of the moment. There's a quirky charm to Ruby that I love. She's optimistic yet insecure, a little humble, which is to be expected for a teenage girl, but it's wonderful to see that in her kraken-self, too."
—Kirk DeMicco, Director

9

10

"Ruby is absolutely adorable, from her design to the voice talent. How she moves, the things that she really cares about, the passion she has—all that works together, and she's just a delight to watch.
  Ruby loves her friends, she loves her life on land, and she's got a good thing going. But the ocean calls to her—there's this weird draw, and she feels a little uncomfortable with the life of lying to her friends, but she is also not very willing to show who she really is. She wants to fit in."
—Glenn Harmon, Head of Story

PROTECT
THE
OCEAN

SEAS THE DAY

1

2

3

4

5

6

7

1, 3, 5, 7: Yuriko Oto • 2, 4, 8–16: Timothy Lamb •
6: animation poses: Carlos Fernandez Puertolas

22

8

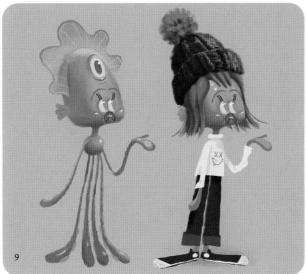

9

10

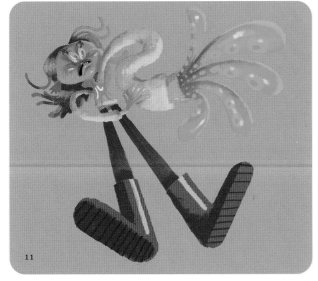

11

12

13

14

15

16

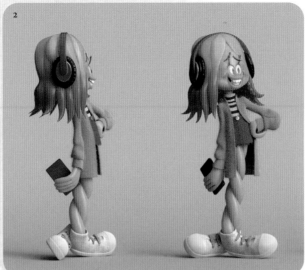

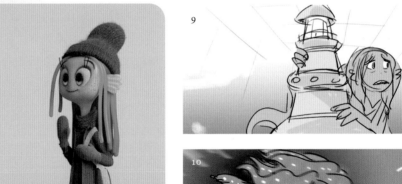

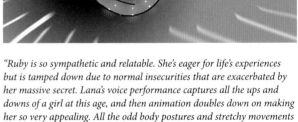

"Ruby is so sympathetic and relatable. She's eager for life's experiences but is tamped down due to normal insecurities that are exacerbated by her massive secret. Lana's voice performance captures all the ups and downs of a girl at this age, and then animation doubles down on making her so very appealing. All the odd body postures and stretchy movements capture a girl already uncomfortable with her own body but even more so when that body becomes truly out of control!"
—MARGIE COHN, PRESIDENT OF DREAMWORKS ANIMATION

"If you connect with Ruby, you relate to the idea that she's been brought up a certain way, and she doesn't have all the information that she feels like she should have. Her parents are trying to protect her, but maybe not going about it the right way and not treating her like an adult who can handle the information. She's just looking for more out of her life. She knows that she's capable of something bigger, so I think the family themes and the mother-daughter dynamics are relatable."
—JON GUTMAN, HEAD OF LAYOUT

11

12

13

14

Agatha

agatha concepts

Agatha loves her life: a wonderful husband, darling children, and a great job. She's well known in the community, her real estate company is successful, and she's managed to hide the fact that under these still waters lurks something deeper and fearsome—but danger is coming! The cracks—or "kraks"—are apparent in the tempestuous relationship she has with her teenage daughter, Ruby, who has been forbidden to go into the ocean. But their relationship is heading for the rocks, as Ruby can't resist the siren song of a party-boat prom on the sea. Agatha's character is tested when Ruby disobeys her "no ocean" command, and to add insult to injury, Agatha's brother, Brill, shows up! Although, it's Uncle Brill who gets injured, as Agatha drives into him with her car.

When Agatha confronts Ruby in her kraken form, we see the kind, empathetic nature of a mother tending to a worried and fearful child, but when we see Agatha confronting titan Nerissa, we see the awesome power of a kraken warrior protecting her own. She's a kraken hero!

1

2

3

4

early concept

5

agatha
hair/head shape
explorations

6

"Mom has left the ocean and is making her life on land and doing everything she can to keep her and her family safe from the dangers present in the ocean. She has one big rule: do not go into the ocean ever, ever, ever. That's the big driving force in her life."
—Glenn Harmon, Head of Story

26

neutral alert happy relieved big smile

7

Agatha
Emotions &
Expressions

confident determined annoyed squash

disheveled frustrated surprised! worried

stretch

8

9 10

27

"Agatha has built herself a business; she's got this house and great family. There's a lot of love between her and her husband, Arthur, but I think the trouble that she has is, like with most parents, there's a conversation that she needs to have with her children, and there's no rule book about the best day or best year to do it. So there's a bit of guilt, and she is carrying around a lot of weight because she knows that her daughter has a superpower. She never calls it a curse. She never looks at it like that; from the get-go, she makes it very clear that she and Ruby are just like Ruby's grandmother. They're gifted this way; they're not monsters."
—KIRK DeMICCO, DIRECTOR

1, 3, 6, 7: GUILLERMO "WILLIE" REAL • 2, 4, 5: TIMOTHY LAMB

"There are small details that we're adding for their skin, but if you get really, really close, you see this subtle dot pattern that we're adding in to give it a little bit of extra detail. This was inspired by some early octopus reference that we were using for inspiration and stylizing."
—MEGAN WALKER, CHARACTER SURFACING SUPERVISOR

"One of our challenges with Agatha, if you're watching the movie from Ruby's point of view, is you think she's overprotective and that she's not letting Ruby live her full life. We wanted to make sure that we still made Agatha empathetic. She would go to any lengths to protect her family—she thought she was protecting Ruby from having to live a life that was going to be mapped out for her, but unfortunately, she ended up doing exactly that: prescribing a life for her."
—KELLY COONEY CILELLA, PRODUCER

"These characters might be sea monsters living in hiding, but ultimately, they're just a family trying to make the best choices they know how, under the circumstances. Even if they don't turn out to be the right choices—like Agatha's choice not to tell Ruby the truth!—they are made with love and good intentions."
—KRISTIN LOWE, CHIEF CREATIVE OFFICER, DREAMWORKS ANIMATION

3

4

5

6

agatha costume hair concepts

7

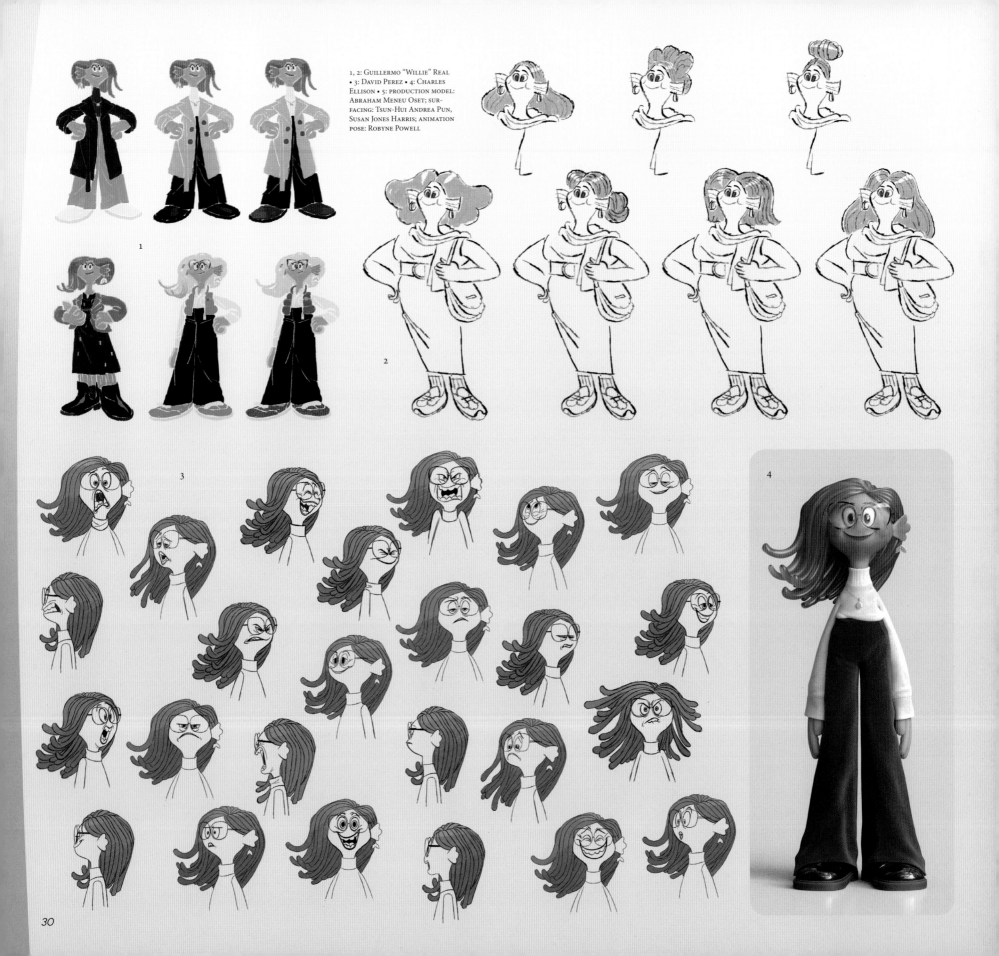

1, 2: Guillermo "Willie" Real • 3: David Perez • 4: Charles Ellison • 5: production model: Abraham Meneu Oset; surfacing: Tsun-Hui Andrea Pun, Susan Jones Harris; animation pose: Robyne Powell

1

2

3

4

"Anyone who's a parent can relate to what Agatha feels: 'I want to keep this thing I love protected, and I want to do everything I can to make it right.' It's not always going to work out perfectly, as it would if she could control everything. But she can't; Agatha has to let go of that control and hope that it's going to be okay."
—Faryn Pearl, Co-Director

"Actress Toni Collette has been able to uncover the humanity under the stern mother, to understand that there's something going on there when she's telling Ruby no. She brings the subtext of a mother's love to every line. When Agatha starts spinning out of control after everything's falling apart, Toni plays up that manic side, so that when she tries to put the genie back in the bottle, she does it with a smile. She brings humor and incredible warmth to the situations and conflicts that she and Ruby are going through. At the lighthouse, without telling Ruby the truth, she's trying her best to connect with her daughter, and you can feel that longing as Toni delivers her lines."
—Kirk DeMicco, Director

"Arthur is a really good person. He's got the best of intentions and tries hard. He loves his wife and his family, and he's just trying to keep things going, but they just keep falling apart."
—GLENN HARMON, HEAD OF STORY

1: GUILLERMO "WILLIE" REAL • 2, 3: CONCEPT MODEL: CHARLES ELLISON • 4: DAVID PEREZ • 5: PRODUCTION MODEL: CATHERIN CUBILLAN REYES; SURFACING: ANDY HARBECK, RACHAEL YANG

Arthur

Solid and dependable, Arthur is the rock on which the family rests. It may be a seaweed-encrusted and barnacled rock, but nonetheless, Arthur is happy to be a reassuring presence for the family—especially considering the impending clash between Agatha and Ruby. As a kraken male, Arthur will never be a warrior of giant stature, heading out to defend the kingdom, but he has a stout heart (and figure to match) and is much loved by his wife and children. He also makes a mean ship-in-a-bottle and owns Oceanside's most bespoke antique shop selling "fintage finiture," "seavenirs," and other curios to the curious but discerning customer.

1

2

3

"Arthur was one of the models that was around very early on. He didn't deviate much as we progressed forward, although we had to solve certain things, because he's got a chin that's full of these fins, and he needs to be able to rotate his head and not have things look incorrect or wrong it or crash."
—DAMON CROWE, HEAD OF CHARACTERS

"I've always found Arthur to be really appealing; it seems like he's just always been there. It feels like his family could always go to him when they need to talk. That's the impression you get—that he's really even-keeled and solid, just from his voice and even in his design; he's like a block."
—FREDERIC WILLIAM STEWART, ART DIRECTOR

4

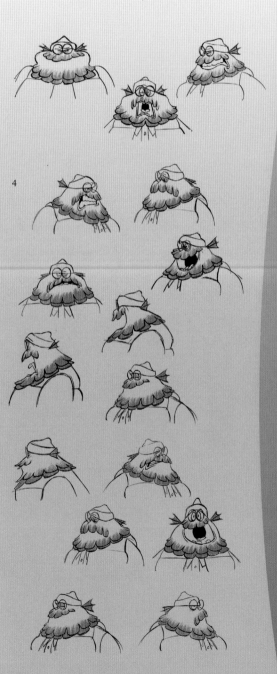

5

Sam

While small, Sam has an outsized personality, and this often gets him into trouble with his big sister, Ruby. He loves sports, albeit swimming is out of the question, but is very good at dodgeball and basketball—although he gets a bit queasy when asked to dunk the ball. He studies hard at school and absorbs information like a sponge, but this precociousness sometimes makes him act out—the little urchin!

3

1

2

4

5

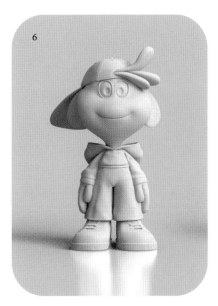

"Sam was a character that went through a bunch of different versions, and he was one of the last ones built and fully realized. Sam became this roughhousing kid, one who annoys his sister but deep down loves her, too."
—Damon Crowe, Head of Characters

1, 2: Guillermo "Willie" Real • 3: Timothy Lamb • 4, 5: production/ lighting images • 6–8: Charles Ellison • 9: production model: Bear Williams; surfacing: Andy Harbeck, Rachael Yang, Lorena Da Silva Pinzón; animation pose: Carlos Fernandez Puertolas

Nessie

Nessie is a baby Loch Ness monster. She's certainly not a purebred, but what she lacks in good manners she more than makes up for with personality. Her coral-colored feet and body barely disguise the prominent gaping maw and purple tongue. Marine biologists have suggested that there is DNA from groupers, angler fish, cephalopods, and lobsters. That's quite the seafood medley, and as such, chefs and restaurant owners are keen to see if Nessie is for sale! Needless to say, the Gillmans have good taste and look after her well. Nessie is walked daily, and sometimes Agatha will let her run around freely with an amused cry of "Unleash the kraken!"

"Nessie is a baby Loch Ness monster with a large mouth, tentacles, and a couple of stalk eyes. She's cute and has a mischievous side to her. She helps Ruby pull one over on her mother, and then later, helps trick Gordon into thinking he's caught a baby kraken."
—Glenn Harmon, Head of Story

1: Guillermo "Willie" Real • 2–5: Timothy Lamb • 6: David Perez • 7–9: production model: Bear Williams; surfacing: Megan Walker; animation pose: Patrick Danaher.

6

7

8

9

Uncle Brill

In the history of embarrassing uncles, Brill is right up there. For one thing, he isn't worried about going "clothes-free" in society, and he also often ends up in somewhat unfortunate predicaments. If something goes wrong, you can bet Uncle Brill (voiced by Sam Richardson) is right there and usually in pain. Ruby's kraken awakening means he must warn his sister, Agatha, that their mother, the kraken queen, is on the warpath! And that's one path Brill would like to travel less.

1

2

uncle brill

uncle brill
covered up

3

4

5

1–9: GUILLERMO "WILLIE" REAL •
10: TOM MACDOUGALL

6

uncle
brill

covered up

birthday
suit

when we
first see
Uncle Brill

7

uncle
brill
costumes

ⓐ the relaxed float

ⓑ artisan, old clothes from the 70s

ⓒ beach sponge

ⓓ comfy confused

8

9

10

"Uncle Brill often takes one for the team, over and over, and that kind of physical humor is always so much fun to explore. Storyboard artists Anthony Holden and Carder Scholin have really capitalized on beating Brill up and finding the comedy in that. It's funny when Uncle Brill gets run over. It's funny when he gets sautéed. It's funny when he gets electrocuted. It's great. We just love it."
—GLENN HARMON, HEAD OF STORY

"Sam Richardson, who plays Uncle Brill, really brings such warmth to this movie, which can sometimes feel on the surface a little bit like there's a lot of interpersonal conflict. It was wonderful to have a character who's genuinely there to see everyone smile. Uncle Brill's goal is for the family to get together. He just wants a hug, and in the end, this movie could be called Brill Gets a Hug from Every Family Member. That's not a good title, but that is what he achieves. I think you're happy to see this very goofy, not-so-quick character really putting in the work to connect on an empathetic level with everyone and succeed in the end. He's the emotional heart of the movie."
—FARYN PEARL, CO-DIRECTOR

1: NEUTRAL MODEL: CATHERIN CUBILLAN
REYES; PRODUCTION MODEL: HANNAH KANG;
SURFACING: BETSY ASHER HALL • 2: PRODUC-
TION MODEL: HANNAH KANG; SURFACING:
BETSY ASHER HALL • 3–5: CONCEPT MODEL:
CHARLES ELLISON • 6: PRODUCTION MODEL:
HANNAH KANG; SURFACING: BETSY ASHER
HALL • OVERLEAF: PIERRE-OLIVIER VINCENT

4

5

6

Part 1

Land

Oceanside

Fair Oceanside! A sight for sore eyes! Set on a sprawling archipelago connected by multiple bridges, there's not a bad site to be found. The largest island is home to Old Town, and other islands and islets hold the docks, schools, neighborhoods, etc. The citizens of Oceanside know they're lucky to live here, and there's a thriving tourist presence. Many come to hear tall tales of kraken monsters from the deep; others come for the sandy beaches and safe surf. Still others come to browse the shops and taste the local seafood treats. Those who live here are happy with their lot, and in general are cheerful and kind. Oceanside's unofficial motto is, "Be the change you wish to sea in the world." Critics have long been fascinated by Oceanside's unique architecture, and there is strong evidence of a French/Viking influence, but you'd have to be a bit of berk to see it. All in all, as the song goes, "Oceanside's the seaside to be beside the sea."

THIS SPREAD: PIERRE-OLIVIER VINCENT, ALEXANDRE PUVILLAND

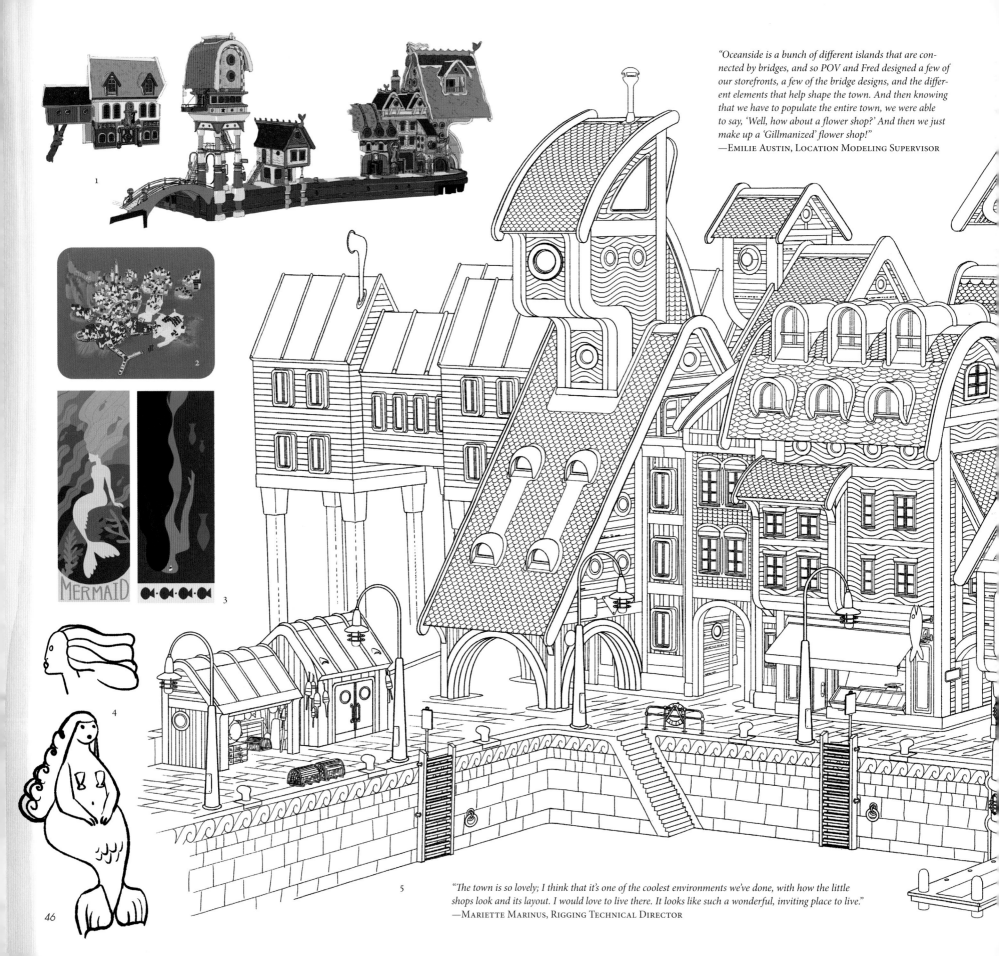

1

2

MERMAID

3

"Oceanside is a bunch of different islands that are connected by bridges, and so POV and Fred designed a few of our storefronts, a few of the bridge designs, and the different elements that help shape the town. And then knowing that we have to populate the entire town, we were able to say, 'Well, how about a flower shop?' And then we just make up a 'Gillmanized' flower shop!"
—EMILIE AUSTIN, LOCATION MODELING SUPERVISOR

4

5

"The town is so lovely; I think that it's one of the coolest environments we've done, with how the little shops look and its layout. I would love to live there. It looks like such a wonderful, inviting place to live."
—MARIETTE MARINUS, RIGGING TECHNICAL DIRECTOR

1: Pierre-Olivier Vincent, Frederic William Stewart • 2: block color: Frederic William Stewart • 3: Yuriko Oto • 4, 5: Pierre-Olivier Vincent

FENCE

BUS STOP

MERMAIDS

1

3 POSITIONS FOUNTAIN

TIDE HORN

FOUNTAINS

2

TIDE HORN

GUTTERS

STREET LIGHTS

STREET CONES

METERS

3

OS POST

OS POST

MAIL BOXES

OCEAN SIDE   OCEAN SIDE   OCEAN SIDE

TRASH CANS

6

5

4

1–3: ALEXANDRE PUVILLAND •
4–6, 9: YURIKO OTO • 7: COLOR
DESIGN: FREDERIC WILLIAM
STEWART • 8: TOM MACDOUGALL •
10: PIERRE-OLIVIER VINCENT • 11:
DESIGN: PIERRE-OLIVIER VINCENT

7

"Oceanside is built on an archipelago. There's a cluster of buildings, and then it connects over to the high school. And by connection, I mean this road that just rests above the water, and then over to the Oceanside Heights, which is a more modern development. The town is what I like the most, because it combines a lot of different styles of architecture. There's a little bit Craftsman, art nouveau, modern, and Scandinavian influence . . . although the high school is made from shipping containers. Everything is inspired by the ocean, of course. There's an aquatic theme that goes throughout everything. I love all the little details that are playful, which could seem childish, but the way we put it together, it creates a place where it's fun for adults to be in that world."
—JASON TURNER, HEAD OF LOCATIONS

8

10

11

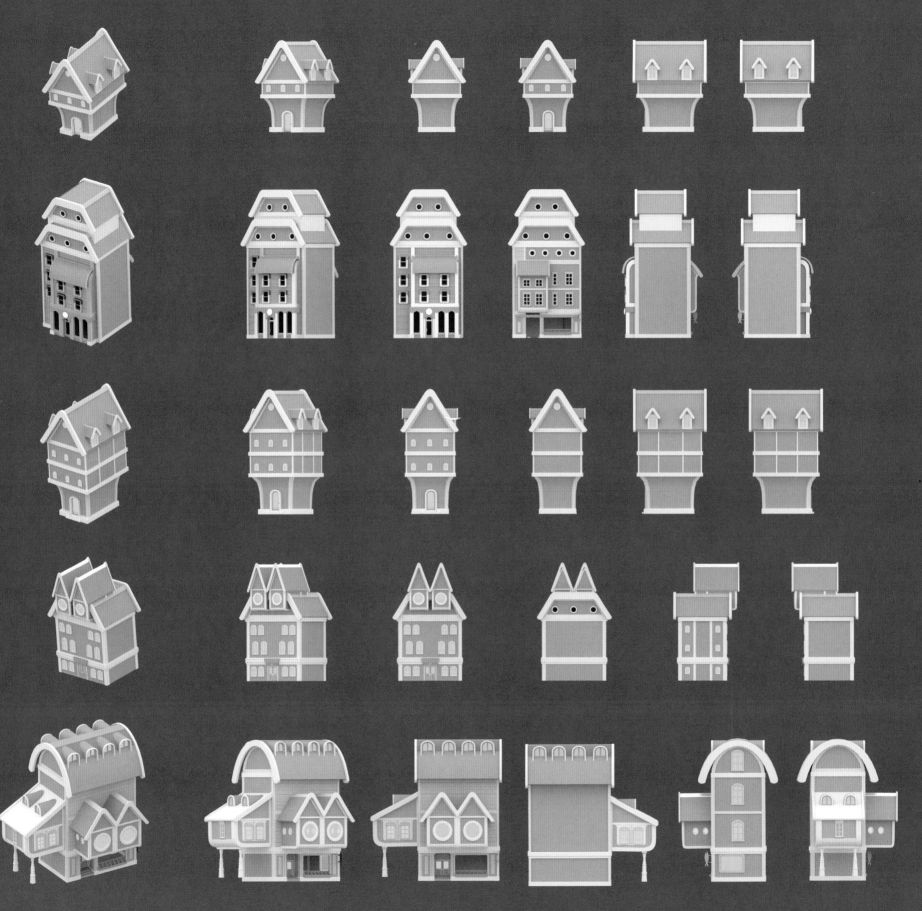

"The town of Oceanside looks like an amusement park. Everything is tubular—from the sconces to the trash cans, everything has been designed with a nautical point of view. It's a marine dreamland. I think Oceanside feels tactile; it almost feels hand-done, like you would see it in any stop-motion movie. It feels like it could all be built in miniature. It feels a little claustrophobic, and it feels cluttered in a really appealing way."
—Faryn Pearl, Co-Director

"It's one of those things people won't think about, but there are lots of flags and banners and ropes and things like that in and around Oceanside. It's got a lot of nautical tie-ins, so we have a system where we do a simulation for each flag just once and then pin that in the background of things so that it can gently waft in the breeze . . . or flags flapping at the top of buildings to give the town more of a maritime look."
—Christopher Michael, CFX Supervisor

Gutter Hangers

2

3

4

5

6

7

8

1–5, 7, 8: Tom MacDougall
• 6: Pierre-Olivier Vincent

51

The Antique Shop

With something for everyone, the Gillmans' antique shop is a must-stop shop when in Oceanside. From nautical knick-knacks to bogus bric-a-brac, from salvaged cannons to charming chests, Arthur Gillman has stocked the floor with a lifetime's haul of treasures. Who he deals with to get the undersea plunder isn't well known. Some whisper that Davy Jones has a good number of lockers, while a shadowy relative called "Uncle Shill" may occasionally sell stuff off the back of a pirate trunk. Whatever the provenance, you will always get a good deal, since Arthur often waves the tax.

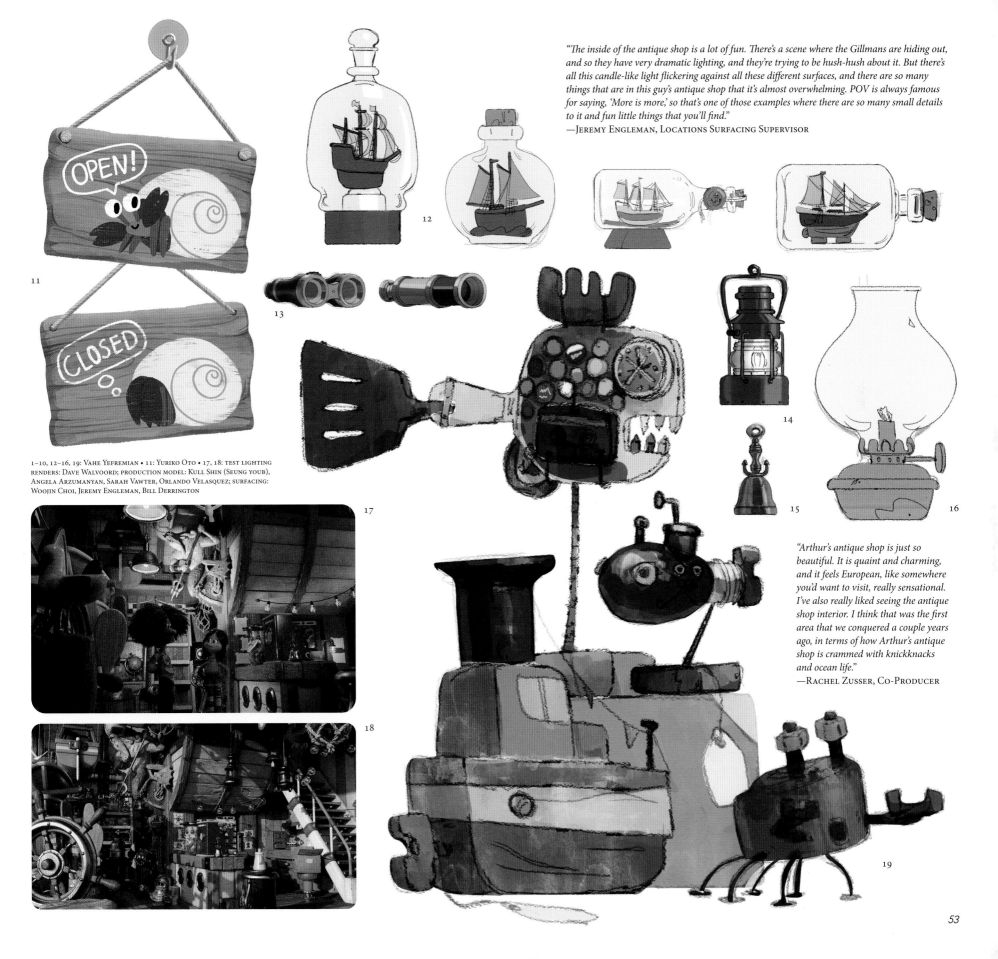

"The inside of the antique shop is a lot of fun. There's a scene where the Gillmans are hiding out, and so they have very dramatic lighting, and they're trying to be hush-hush about it. But there's all this candle-like light flickering against all these different surfaces, and there are so many things that are in this guy's antique shop that it's almost overwhelming. POV is always famous for saying, 'More is more,' so that's one of those examples where there are so many small details to it and fun little things that you'll find."
—Jeremy Engleman, Locations Surfacing Supervisor

1–10, 12–16, 19: Vahe Yefremian • 11: Yuriko Oto • 17, 18: test lighting renders: Dave Walvoord; production model: Kull Shin (Seung youb), Angela Arzumanyan, Sarah Vawter, Orlando Velasquez; surfacing: Woojin Choi, Jeremy Engleman, Bill Derrington

"Arthur's antique shop is just so beautiful. It is quaint and charming, and it feels European, like somewhere you'd want to visit, really sensational. I've also really liked seeing the antique shop interior. I think that was the first area that we conquered a couple years ago, in terms of how Arthur's antique shop is crammed with knickknacks and ocean life."
—Rachel Zusser, Co-Producer

The Gillmans' House

It might not be to everyone's taste, but the Gillmans' house is a thing of beauty. It's a four-story marvel. The ground floor encompasses the antique shop (where you can, in fact, buy compasses), while the second floor is where the kitchen and living rooms are. The third floor has the master bedroom and two smaller bedrooms (one is for Sam) and a bathroom. The top floor is where Ruby has her bedroom and bathroom. No expense was spared on details. Note the many varieties of shingles as well as old brass cornices, interesting color schemes, and, of course, a lovely old weather vane. Just minutes from the old quay and downtown shopping, this house is perfect for the family that wants to stay out of sight in plain sight.

It's one of the older houses in town and has an interesting history. It is said that it was used by smugglers and pirates many years ago, which may account for some of the antiques found in Arthur's shop. There's a doorbell, as the siren was felt to be too loud, and much shiplap flooring throughout. All in all, the Gillmans find it accommodates them very well indeed.

1

2

3

"The Gillmans live in this house by the harbor where everything is marine-driven, and there's even a little callback to what was probably their previous life underwater. You can see that everything inside the house is always decorated with a bit of a wavy motif. There are a lot of blues, a lot of cool colors with a few color splashes, but I think it's very ocean-y, and that tower Ruby lives in looks a little bit like an old-style Martha's Vineyard lighthouse. Her bedroom has a giant window (or oculus), and what she sees is the sea. Everything has to constantly remind you of that. It's true for a lot of people that are living in exile—they're trying to re-create something that reminds them of their cultural origins, and for the Gillmans, it's the ocean."
—Pierre-Olivier Vincent,
Production Designer

1, 4: Pierre-Olivier Vincent
2: production model render: Ming Hao Yu; surfacing: Woojin Choi • 3: production model render: Angela Arzumanyan, Emmanuel Marenco, Emilie Austin, Erin Caswell; surfacing: Woojin Choi, Jeremy Engleman, Sara V. Cembalisty

4

Living Quarters

If form follows function, then the Gillmans have form. Everything in the house is curved and accessible. Agatha has an eye for the comforting and comfortable, and the living quarters are a wonderful haven of peace and tranquility. Having escaped a life as a warrior queen, Agatha has made sure her house is different from the coldly magnificent palace of her youth. A Canadian's house is her castle (moat not included), and this one is warm and inviting.

"Everything has a chunkiness to it, down to something as simple as a couch cushion or something small that rests on the table. Nothing is really sharp, and in this case, it's chunky and round. That's the style, and so it's inviting and nonthreatening. Everything has a whimsy to it that way."
—JASON TURNER, HEAD OF LOCATIONS

"I love the breakfast scene where they're all eating, the chaos of it all. Obviously, these are krakens, but it's so relatable just as a human experience."
—MIKE MURRAY, SUPERVISING TECHNICAL DIRECTOR

2

1, 2, 9: ALEXANDRE PUVILLAND • 3, 6–8: PIERRE-OLIVIER VINCENT • 4, 5: PRODUCTION MODEL: JAEWON LEE, KOJI TSUKAMOTO; SURFACING: SARA V. CEMBALISTY • 10: PRODUCTION MODEL: JAEWON LEE; SURFACING: SARA V. CEMBALISTY • OVERLEAF: PRODUCTION MODEL: JAEWON LEE; SURFACING: SARA V. CEMBALISTY

3

1

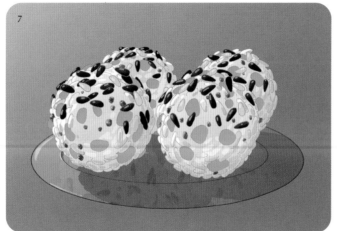

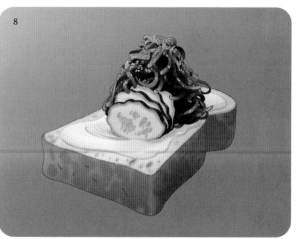

RAFTER IMPRINTS

Ruby's Room

As any teenage girl's room should be, it's a mess, but at least Ruby knows where everything is. From her favorite posters on the wall to her homework buried on the desk, there's a place for everything and everything in its "plaice." Ruby has a great view through her window of the ocean and from time to time will wonder what lies below the horizon. It's just one of many questions she has about the future, and if she can avoid her mother's entreaties to clean up her room, she might just have to have them answered.

1 KEEP OUR OCEANS CLEAN
SAY NO TO PLASTIC

2 live in concert
OCEAN'S DAUGHTERS
for Ruby XO XO J Lamia
26 27 28
3 SHOWS at the

1, 4–7: Yuriko Oto • 2, 3: Pierre-Olivier Vincent • 8: production model: Emilie Austin; surfacing: Sara V. Cembalisty • 9: production model: Emilie Austin; surfacing: Sara V. Cembalisty

3 PROM

4

shelf   chair   plant
desk

"Ruby's room is a real standout for me. There's all these plushy little pillows and bedding, and there's just a lot of rich surfaces that beg to be explored."
—Jeremy Engleman, Locations Surfacing Supervisor

"Ruby's bedroom, for me, just felt like I was catapulted back to my youth—how great the posters on the wall look and the clutter on the desk. I could relate to this 100 percent. And she's got the coolest bedroom of all. She's got this great lookout point; she sees the whole ocean from her window. It's fantastic."
—Rachel Zusser, Co-Producer

The Pier

When Ruby feels high school is tough, and there's too much "pier pressure," she can often be found at the town pier looking wistfully out at the ocean. One day after accidentally knocking Connor into the water, she has to dive in and rescue him. Alas, her kraken self makes an appearance, and she now must run and hide for fear of discovery.

"There are lots of seagulls in the movie; we're putting them everywhere we can. There are little Easter eggs of seagulls wherever we can fit them in. We'll put a seagull in a locker, or the seagull will be in the school, and they'll follow the people as if they're one of them. They'll be taking walks right next to them. The directors are so supportive. Some of these things, you never know if they'll make it in the movie, but we're very much encouraged to say, 'Oh, the seagulls,' when they're all doing those snapshots at the end, and they'll all be doing their 'Oh, these are our photo booth poses.' You just always have to keep finding that space."
—DAVID BAZELON, CROWD SUPERVISOR

1: FREDERIC WILLIAM STEWART • 2: YURIKO OTO • 3–6: ALEXANDRE PUVILLAND • 7: TIMOTHY LAMB

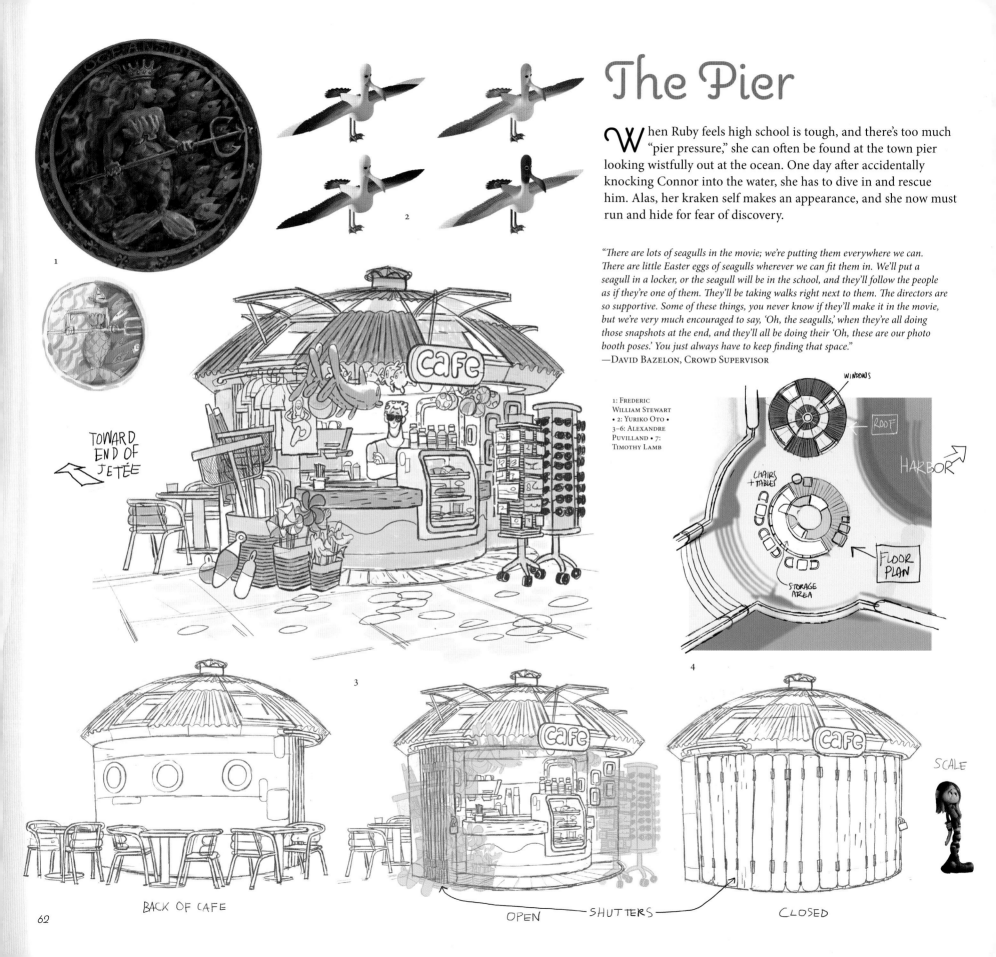

TOWARD END OF JETÉE

WINDOWS

ROOF

HARBOR

CHAIRS + TABLES

FLOOR PLAN

STORAGE AREA

1

2

3

4

BACK OF CAFE

OPEN

SHUTTERS

CLOSED

SCALE

"For lighting, I think there's a richness and depth that they have given each scene. The scene when Ruby jumps off the boardwalk . . . the lighting had to show that was her real moment of choosing to break out of her status quo. There's this gorgeous shot where the lights really paved the way to where she needs to go, which is the ocean."
—FARYN PEARL, CO-DIRECTOR

The Docks

Oceanside may be a beautiful archipelago connected to the mainland via stunning bridges, but it's also a hardworking port. Down at the docks, the town gives way to a grittier side where goods are stored and moved and the tourists stay away. Ruby has never been allowed to hang out here (the hangars are too close to the water's edge), but after saving Oceanside, she is awarded the "quays" to the city by the grateful citizens who now harbor no illusions that monsters exist.

1

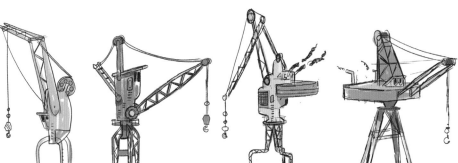

2

3

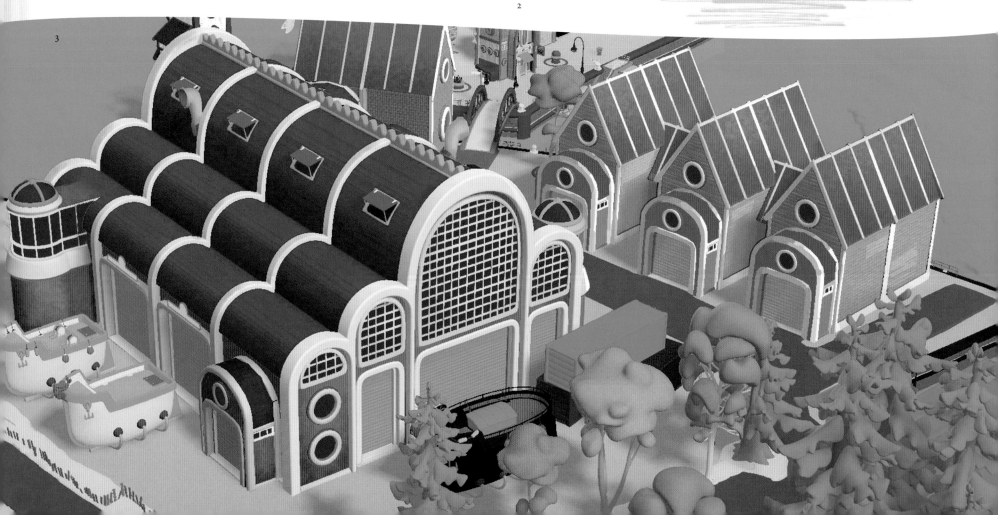

4

"We apply the same kind of stylization to everything in the city. All the cars and boats are a little bit chubby and small. We made everything a little bit roundish, and then, because there was this underwater theme, I decided that maybe the town could be treated as a little reef, and the first thing you notice when you look at a beautiful coral reef is all the colors. Therefore, we are using a very saturated palette for all the buildings. It's also full of patterns everywhere. The wood has different kinds of grain patterns. The cladding on the buildings follows a wavy pattern as well, and everything is a little bit softer. We're also using some surprising elements, like brass or even gold-like material, to be part of the architecture and give it a little bit of a shine. A lot of the fish that you can see are very complex in their patterns and textures. All of this helps create a little parallel world that still has the complexity of what you might expect from a real place but also makes it a little bit more stylized, like something a bit special that can support, firstly, the presence of our sea monsters in there and something a little bit more charming and comedic."
—Pierre-Olivier Vincent, Production Designer

1, 2, 5: Alexandre Puvilland • 3: production model: Emilie Austin, Erin Caswell; color: Yuriko Oto • 4: production model: Emilie Austin, Erin Caswell; surfacing: Woojin Choi

5

Oceanside Heights

Echo location, location, location. Oceanside Heights has it all. Great views, easy access to downtown, ocean frontage, and state-of-the-art architecture all combine for a place to buy the perfect starter home. Agatha Gillman (owner of Gillman Real Estate) loves selling here, and as long as you look past the teenage kraken that occasionally wanders through, it's a very quiet neighborhood. The houses have been stress-tested for tsunamis and other natural disasters, but kraken damage is unfortunately not covered by insurance.

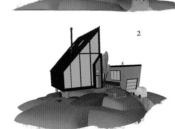

2

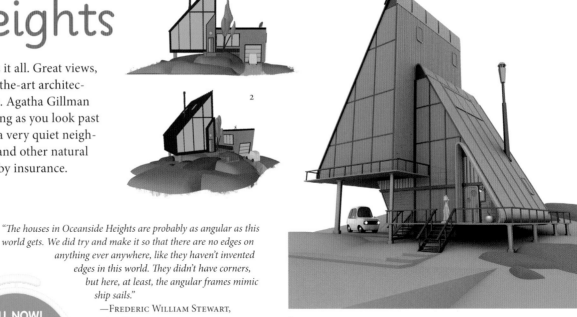

"The houses in Oceanside Heights are probably as angular as this world gets. We did try and make it so that there are no edges on anything ever anywhere, like they haven't invented edges in this world. They didn't have corners, but here, at least, the angular frames mimic ship sails."
—Frederic William Stewart, Art Director

3

Your Dream Island Life

GILLMAN REAL ESTATE

CALL NOW!
AGATHA GILLMAN
555-0100

1

5

4

1: Yuriko Oto • 2, 3, 5–7: Tom MacDougall • 4: Pierre-Olivier Vincent

"Agatha is the best at blending in and being human, and she's very successful as a realtor. We were trying to portray—before everything goes wrong—that she is a good mother and a good realtor, somebody that you would actually buy a house from. She's very charming but very professional."
—CARLOS FERNANDEZ PUERTOLAS, HEAD OF ANIMATION

OceanSide
Estates
Demo
House

1

GARDEN

2

OceanSide
Estates

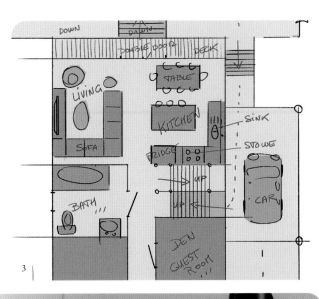

3

DOWN
DOWN
DOUBLE DOOR
DECK
LIVING
TABLE
SOFA
KITCHEN
SINK
FRIDGE
STOVE
UP
BATH
UP
CAR
DEN
GUEST
ROOM

4

5

6

7

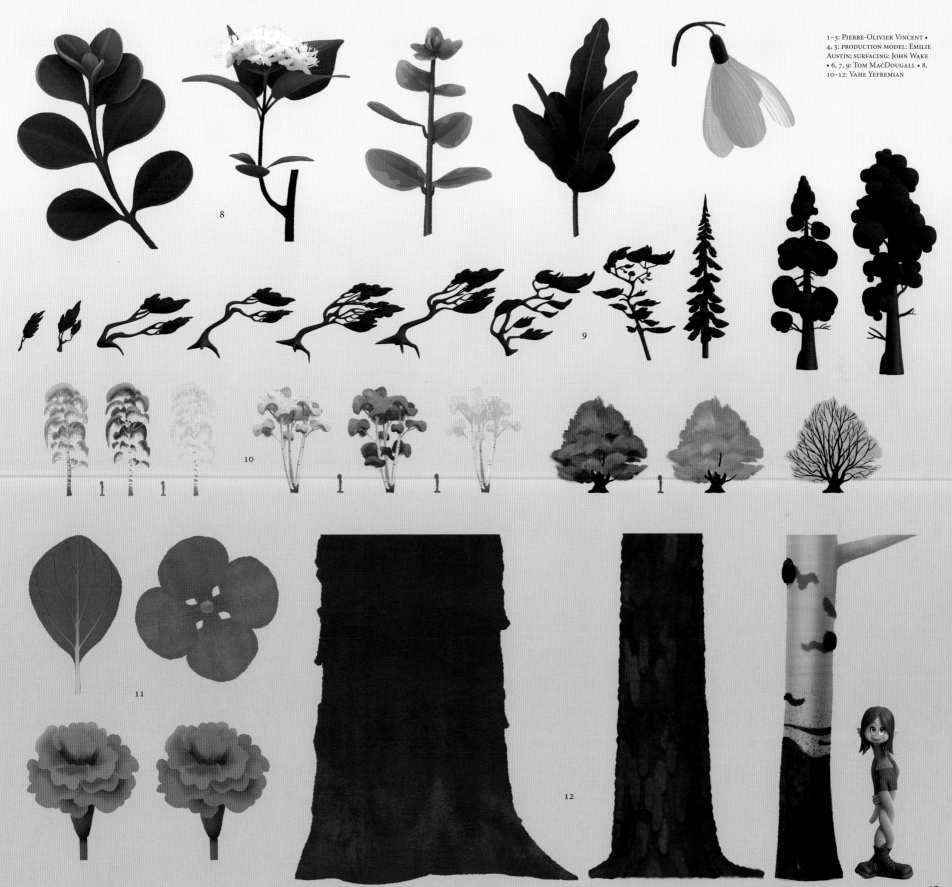

1–3: Pierre-Olivier Vincent • 4, 5: production model: Emilie Austin; surfacing: John Wake • 6, 7, 9: Tom MacDougall • 8, 10–12: Vahe Yefremian

8

9

10

11

12

Connor

The object of Ruby's affections but never affected, Connor (voiced by Jaboukie Young-White) is one cool sea cucumber. Often seen around town with his skateboard and curtain of curly hair, Connor faces the world (which is quite tricky with all that hair) with an openness and earnestness that endears him to all. When rescued by Ruby from a watery grave, he isn't quite sure what happened and in the days following is unable to put two and two together. Fortunately, all is revealed when Ruby saves the day, and she and Connor can go to the prom after all. Then their relationship is "offishial"!

"We didn't want to make Connor your classic kind of sport guy; we wanted to create the new version of that. We've created this charming skater guy who is very friendly and not a bully. He's just such a nice, charming guy. And I think that really works for Connor. Everybody really likes Connor when they meet him."
—Carlos Fernandez Puertolas, Head of Animation

1

2

3

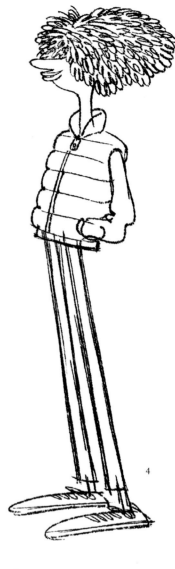

4

1–4: Craig Kellman •
5, 6, 8: Timothy Lamb •
7: Kerry McAllister

5

6

"I've always told people: to do story artist work is to do the comic-book version of the movie, because we're not animators—that's one of the big misconceptions. People think if you're a story artist, then you're an animator or that you write the story, and neither one is true. We take the script from the writer, take a pitch—just a sequence, just a little chunk, four or five pages—and we draw out the comic-book version of the movie, and with that, we're exploring the jokes. We're exploring the environment. We're exploring the character. And those are the things that we try to bring to the table. We'll give that to that artist and say, 'You just run with it. Come up with something; think outside of the box; go crazy.' If it's something more action-driven, maybe there will be some dialogue and even some specific notes of where to go action-wise, where it needs to do this, since we have certain plot points we need to hit, but even in that case, that story artist brings a lot of cinematography, a lot of vitality through cutting. They must be a good editor, a good artist, and have to think about motivations and how the characters think. This leads me to the other things we think about: character, drama, action, and comedy. Every artist has a little chunk of each of those things, but it varies. It's for us to know, 'Oh, we've got this action scene. It's very heavy. This guy can do it,' or 'She's the perfect comedian for that.'"
—GLENN HARMON, HEAD OF STORY

7

8

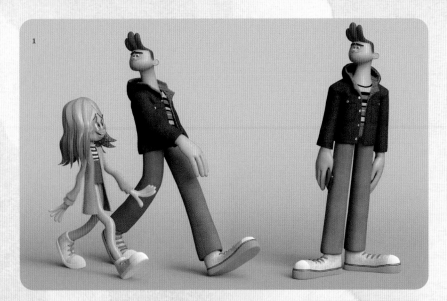

"Connor was fun, because we knew his hair was going to drive a large aspect of his personality. We did a lot of early experimentation on Connor's type of hair. What is curly hair in this world? We even, at one point, had hair that we called spaghetti hair, which was more tubes, almost stop-motion-looking spaghetti hair! We went through many different versions of that and even pushed for colors, like purple hair, and other pieces to find the sweet spot for Connor, because Connor and Ruby always needed to work well with each other."
—DAMON CROWE, HEAD OF CHARACTERS

"I love Ruby's awkward courtship with Connor. They're so wonderfully and sweetly nervous around each other, and the filmmakers did such a wonderful job with this scene that you can really feel each character's nervousness and trepidation all mixed up with the excitement of a first crush."
—KRISTIN LOWE, CHIEF CREATIVE OFFICER, DREAMWORKS ANIMATION

1, 2, 6, 7: Charles Ellison • 3, 4: production model: Bear Williams; surfacing: Betsy Asher Hall, Andy Harbeck, Jeannie Yip Cho, Megan Walker • 5: production model: Bear Williams; surfacing: Rachael Yang • 8: Pierre-Olivier Vincent

Squad Solidarity

Margot (voiced by Liza Koshy), Bliss (voiced by Ramona Young), and Trevin (voiced by Eduardo Franco) make up three-quarters of the "squad." Ruby is the fourth member, and thus, it ought to be the "squid," but that's one secret she's not telling her friends, which is a shame, as all three are smarter and more empathetic than they look! Margot is the extrovert with a dress sense to shame a rainbow; Bliss is the introvert with a penchant for the gothic; and Trevin is the gamer with his head buried in a screen. The four friends have found one another and stick together through thick and "fin." Ruby is the de facto leader in the group, so when she goes missing while a monster is seen at the high school, the squad can't believe she doesn't know anything about it. When Ruby's true nature is finally revealed, the squad rally in her support.

1, 3, 4: Timothy Lamb • 2: Pierre-Olivier Vincent (as Ruby Gillman) • 5: Production render

GAMER-TREVIN

FEATRE MARGO

BLISS WORRIER

RUBY.

MARGOT.

BLISS.

TREVIN.

4

"All our clothing is actually knit or woven; we didn't do the cheap thing that we've all done for years, where you just model a solid shirt and put a texture on it. With Bliss, there's a shot where the lights are behind her, and her shirt is sheer, and you can see her shadow right through it."
—DAVE WALVOORD, VFX SUPERVISOR

MARGOT.

"A lot of Margot lives in the surfacing—the colors of her outfit, her hair, all of these pieces—and she's so flamboyant. She's definitely a theatrical person!"
—Damon Crowe, Head of Characters

1

2

3

4

5

6

"*Margot is as colorful, as bright, as in-your-face as we can make her. I put a lot of my love of 1970s musical theater into her—I mean, her prom outfit is a sequined tuxedo!*"
—Faryn Pearl, Co-Director

1, 5: Julien Le Rolland • 2–4, 6, 9, 12–14: Yuriko Oto • 7: production model: Abraham Meneu Oset • 8: Pierre-Olivier Vincent (as Ruby Gillman) • 10: design: Julien Le Rolland; color: Yuriko Oto • 11: production model: Abraham Meneu Oset; surfacing: Andy Harbeck, Rachael Yang, Tsun-Hui Andrea Pun; animation pose: Anthony Hodgson

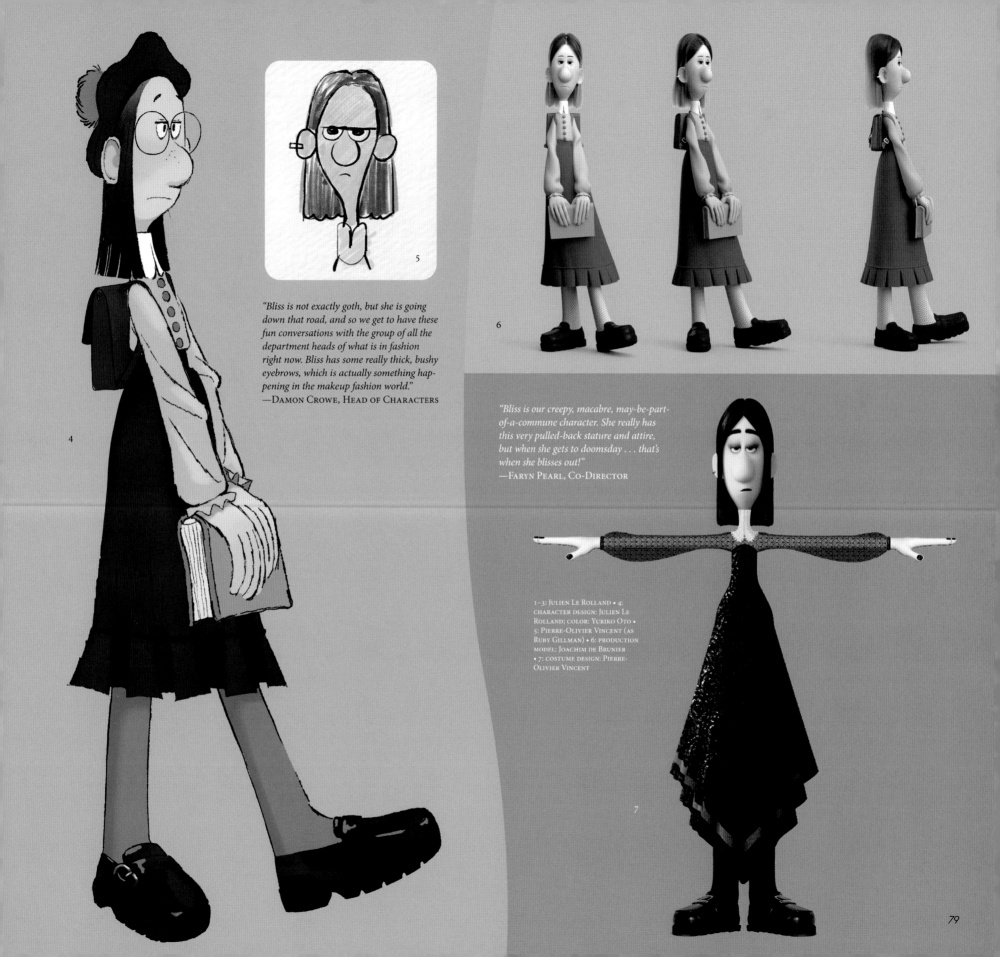

"Bliss is not exactly goth, but she is going down that road, and so we get to have these fun conversations with the group of all the department heads of what is in fashion right now. Bliss has some really thick, bushy eyebrows, which is actually something happening in the makeup fashion world."
—DAMON CROWE, HEAD OF CHARACTERS

"Bliss is our creepy, macabre, may-be-part-of-a-commune character. She really has this very pulled-back stature and attire, but when she gets to doomsday . . . that's when she blisses out!"
—FARYN PEARL, CO-DIRECTOR

1–3: JULIEN LE ROLLAND • 4: CHARACTER DESIGN: JULIEN LE ROLLAND; COLOR: YURIKO OTO • 5: PIERRE-OLIVIER VINCENT (AS RUBY GILLMAN) • 6: PRODUCTION MODEL: JOACHIM DE BRUNIER • 7: COSTUME DESIGN: PIERRE-OLIVIER VINCENT

TREVIN.

"I think that the way the squad has come together is fun to watch. They're a little pack of misfits. It feels like they've known each other for a while, they grew up together, and they have rapport."
—FREDERIC WILLIAM STEWART, ART DIRECTOR

"Trevin is our most modern character in a way—a guy who just looks at his video games and his console all day. We had a big discussion on whether we should ever see his eyes. Hopefully, by the end of the movie, you're going to see those beautiful, beautiful peepers of his, but I love how the art department really made his whole form feel hunched, like he belongs in a video game. He also has a very wonderful simulated-reality-themed prom outfit in the end; he really feels like part of the code. We wanted to lean into the fact that social media is a huge part of how teens and even families connect—or feel disconnected. It just felt like an opportunity for us, more than anything else."
—FARYN PEARL, CO-DIRECTOR

1–4, 10–12: TIMOTHY LAMB
• 5–9: FREDERIC WILLIAM STEWART

1

2

3

4

Chelsea Van der Zee

She's the popular new girl at the high school, and when Ruby first sees her, she's mesmerized and dearly wants to fit in as effortlessly as Chelsea (voiced by Annie Murphy) does. Quite what she sees in her, apart from her glamorous looks, popularity, and wealth, is hard to fathom, but Chelsea has her eyes on Ruby, too—so the two do indeed become besties. Or should that be "beasties," as Chelsea is also hiding a secret? She is a mermaid (sworn enemies of krakens) but seems so friendly, even saving Ruby from an attack by Gordon. They were clearly "mer-made" to be BFFs! Can the relationship avoid being shipwrecked, or will she jump ship? Chelsea has her sights set on the Trident of Oceanus and will stop at nothing to get it—even if that means betraying Ruby.

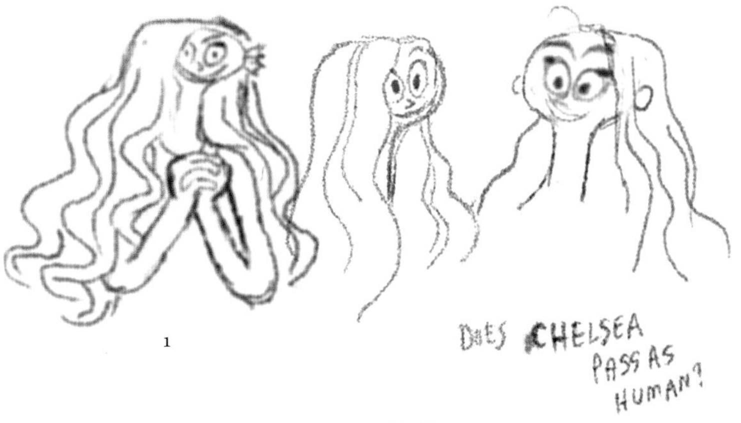

1

DOES CHELSEA PASS AS HUMAN?

2

3

"For Chelsea, we knew that she still had to be the prettiest girl in school. You still had to fully buy into that world when you meet her. She was built very similarly, across the board, as all the other characters, but in the design process, you had to know that there was a dial you could tweak to make her go evil."
—Damon Crowe, Head of Characters

1–3, 5: Timothy Lamb • 4: character design: Julien Le Rolland; color: Yuriko Oto

1: Julien Le Rolland • 2, 3: Charles Ellison • 4, 5: production model: Joachim de Brunier; surfacing: Andy Harbeck, Rachael Yang, Megan Walker; animation pose: Mark Roennigke

2

3

4

"The fun part is being able to help with the design of the characters, bringing them to life, working really closely with the character designers, and trying to create something extremely appealing for a wide audience. Because this movie is on a slightly faster track, there wasn't as much artwork, and what that meant was that the art department bled into modeling, surfacing, and lighting. We got the opportunity to explore and use our art sense to bring these characters to life. For instance, we had to redesign Chelsea in her human form, because the initial artwork wasn't quite right, and POV just said, 'Hey, give it a pass. I'm not going to do a drawing; you guys bring in your sensibility.'"
—BEAR WILLIAMS, CHARACTER MODELING SUPERVISOR

5

1: DESIGN: JULIEN LE ROLLAND; COLOR: YURIKO OTO
• 2, 3: JULIEN LE ROLLAND • 4: CONCEPT MODEL:
CHARLES ELLISON • 5: PRODUCTION MODEL: JOACHIM
DE BRUNIER; SURFACING: JEANNIE YIP CHO, MEGAN
WALKER; ANIMATION POSE: MARK ROENNIGKE

1

2

3

"In the very, very early version of this movie, I thought it was too obvious that Chelsea was a villain. Is it a problem to know that the villain is the villain? No, not if the character is still entertaining and fun. The challenge in this movie is that we are playing with this balancing act—we don't know whether Chelsea is evil or not, and it all relates back to the protagonist, which is Ruby. If the audience knows that this girl is bad, and then Ruby doesn't notice that behavior, it will just weaken Ruby's character, which was the main issue. The fun is in staying on that line for as long as you can. And I think that's what we're going for."
—CARLOS FERNANDEZ PUERTOLAS,
HEAD OF ANIMATION

The High School

Oceanside's high school is clearly not your average school—it's in a class by itself. Constructed from recycled shipping containers, it contains the best and brightest students, but it can't contain a certain teenager with the power to become a kraken—the poor school-library roof is proof of this. Students are very proud of the school band, which used to be out of "tuna," but are now very catchy, with a good "bass" drumline and a "flambuoyant" use of "cast-a-nets."

1: CONCEPT MODEL: PIERRE-OLIVIER VINCENT • 2, 3: PRODUCTION MODEL RENDER: EMILIE AUSTIN; SURFACING: SARA V. CEMBALISTY • 4: VY TRINH • 5: PRODUCTION MODEL RENDER: JAEWON LEE, EMILIE AUSTIN, ANGELA ARZUMANYAN, HYUN HUH, ERIN CASWELL; SURFACING: SARA V. CEMBALISTY, JOHN WAKE • 6: PRODUCTION MODEL RENDER: JAEWON LEE, ANGELA ARZUMANYAN; SURFACING: JOHN WAKE

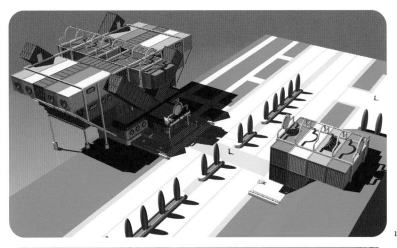

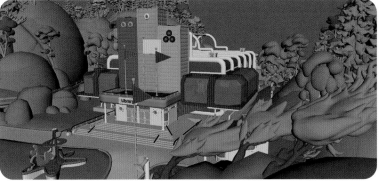

School Life

In a promising turn of events, the students are going crazy for prom. "Promposals" are happening every other minute, and the air is full of half-crazed hormones! The hallways are lined with lockers (not Davy Jones's), and on every wall are posters exhorting students to care for the environment. Students are asked to "seas the day" and live a "porpoiseful life." It's a great school where "anyfin" is possible!

1

CONNER

RUBY

GEOMETRIC NOSES! (NOT ANATOMICAL NOSES)

2

3

ALL ABOARD
PROM

4

5

6

1, 6: Timothy Lamb •
2–5, 7, 9–11 : Frederic
William Stewart • 8:
Yuriko Oto, Frederic
William Stewart •
overleaf: Alexandre
Puvilland

7

8

9

10

"The high school is fantastic. I love the 'promposal' sequence. When Ruby and friends are inside the high school and they're walking through the hallway and seeing all these amazing 'promposals' . . . it's a really fun, fresh way of saying, 'Yeah, this is how we relate to the kids these days; this is what high school is about.'"
—Rachel Zusser, Co-Producer

11

1, 2: MODEL RENDER: EMILIE AUSTIN; SURFACING: JOHN WAKE • 3–5: MODEL RENDER: SARAH VAWTER, ORLANDO VELASQUEZ; SURFACING: WOOJIN CHOI • 6: TEST LIGHTING RENDER: JOHN WAKE, DAVE WALVOORD; MODEL: JAEWON LEE; SURFACING: JOHN WAKE • 7: YURIKO OTO

OHS WATERPOLO
GAME DAY
OCEANSIDE MERMAIDS VS SANDYBEACH SARDINES
APR 30
STARTS 7PM
OHS POOL

Swim with the Big Fish

OHS HONOR SOCIETY

OHS DRAMA presents...
MOBY DICK
May 5, 6, 11, 12 @ 7PM
May 13 @ 2PM
at Oceanside Theater

Join the ECO-CLUB
First Monday every Month! @ Room 206
SAVE OUR PLANET!

SCUBA CLUB
Meetings every 3rd Tuesday @ Room 218
Join our Local Dives!
Every First Saturday
time/place TBD

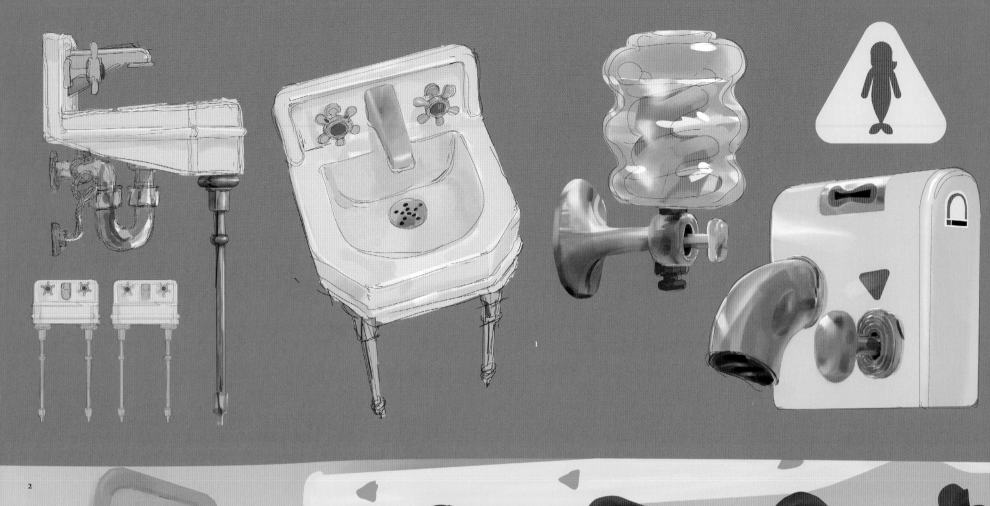

1

2

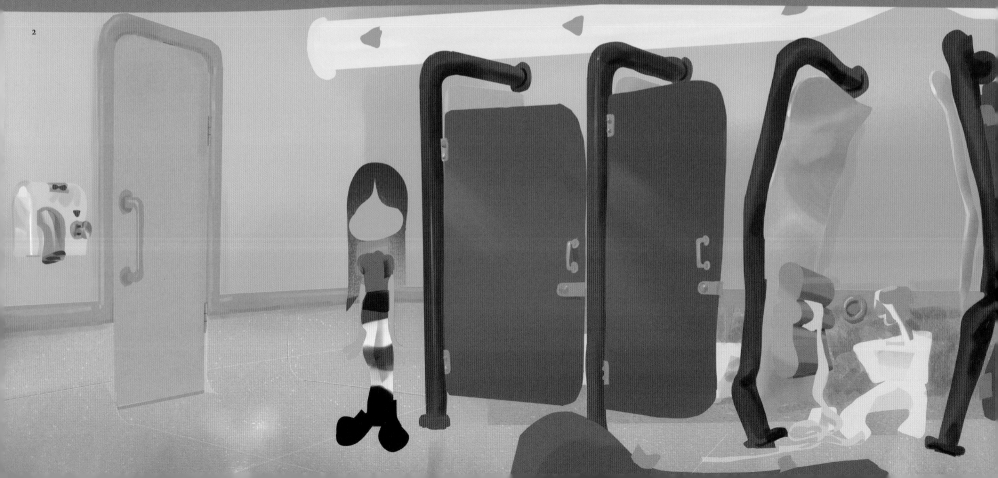

TEEN TO MONSTER TRANSFORMATION!
— HULKING OUT OF HER CLOTHES IN THE H.S. BATHROOM

3

4

"People respond to Ruby's dilemma from different perspectives. High school is a time when differences can be magnified, and we've heard from audiences that Ruby accepting herself as a giant kraken was similar to their own journeys—being the only person of color or other ethnic descent in school, being queer and not yet out, being an immigrant struggling with a new language, having a disability, or just growing a foot taller before everyone else. So many people feel that they are different in some way, and this story of self-acceptance resonated."
—Margie Cohn, President of DreamWorks Animation

"It's been such a pleasure working with POV and Fred. I think that the world we created is so whimsical and fun, and the renders are looking so beautiful. POV and Fred were fantastic at giving us a lot of amazing designs and then also giving us the opportunity to, within the confines of the world and the rules of the world, design, shape, and language-making, bring our own creative take on some things."
—Emilie Austin, Location Modeling Supervisor

1, 2: Frederic William Stewart • 3, 4: Timothy Lamb • 5: test lighting render & surfacing: Dave Walvoord, John Wake; modeling: Koji Tsukamoto

5

"Ruby represents something that everyone can empathize with. They could see themselves, or they've experienced a similar feeling—just like in high school or grade school—where you're the new kid in town, or you're a little bit different than everybody else. And there are times where you try very hard to fit in, but things just don't click, and you still feel like you're an outsider or that you don't belong, or you've been excluded for a certain reason."
—David Valera, Final Layout Supervisor

The School Library

At a remove from the main buildings, the school library sits isolated, which is perfect for those students who want somewhere quiet to check out. Ruby ends up transforming into her kraken "shelf" and has to book it if she wants to avoid detection by the school librarian. As a kraken, she swaps the bookshelves for the continental shelf and desperately flees the building for better cover.

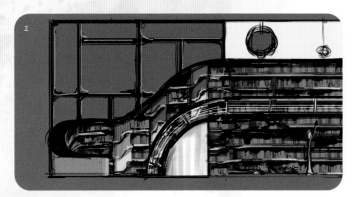

1: PRODUCTION RENDER MODEL: EMILIE AUSTIN; SURFACING: SARA V. CEMBALISTY • 2–11: FREDERIC WILLIAM STEWART

"Once into the second act, we're dealing with an adventure movie and all that kind of action, but I really like that poor Ruby has her life turned upside down and becomes a monster—the little moment in high school where Ruby tries to hide from everybody and goes to the darkest corner in the library, but just explodes into a kraken. She's in a high school built of steel containers, but we never actually cage her—but it is the closest thing to being in a cage. It's a fun kind of disruptive—she breaks out because she's so scared, but she's not a threat to others. She rips herself out of a metal prison, balloons go flying, and the librarian's running away with the book cart. It becomes a centerpiece for the film: what blew up the library?"
—KIRK DeMICCO, DIRECTOR

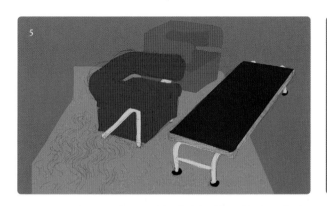

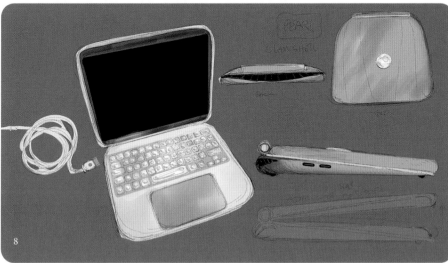

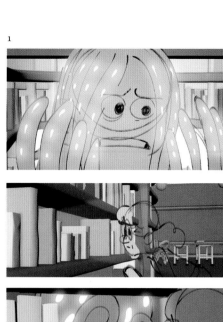

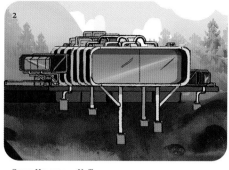

1: Glenn Harmon • 2: Vy Trinh • 3–5: rough layout renders: Dave Walvoord, Koji Tsukamoto, Pil Gyu Chang, and Angela Arzumanyan; previz: Nicola Rinciari; animation prep: Andy Long; set dressing: Ellen Harris; final camera: JC Alvarez • 6, 7: previz: Jon Gutman; animation prep: Andy Long; set dressing: Ellen Harris; final camera: JC Alvarez • 8: prom preparation concept: Yuriko Oto • overleaf: Pierre-Olivier Vincent

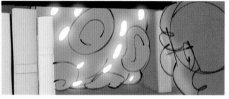

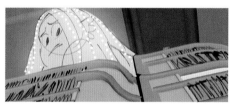

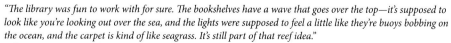

"The library was fun to work with for sure. The bookshelves have a wave that goes over the top—it's supposed to look like you're looking out over the sea, and the lights were supposed to feel a little like they're buoys bobbing on the ocean, and the carpet is kind of like seagrass. It's still part of that reef idea."
—FREDERIC WILLIAM STEWART, ART DIRECTOR

8

Gordon Lighthouse

Gordon (voiced by Will Forte) puts the "arrr" in "krarrrken," as well as "barrrmy," but that doesn't stop him from running a fairly successful tour-bus company and manning Oceanside's historic lighthouse. Together with his trusted "parrrtner," Crab Davey, he roams Oceanside, as well as the ocean (the tour bus is amphibious), looking for evidence of mysterious marine monsters. He keeps a close watch on the Gillmans, as he senses something fishy about the family, but while they seem a little off-color, he can't pin down what exactly they're hiding. Although "cantankarrrous," (some would say crabby, but that would upset his sidekick) when provided with proof that monsters *do* exist, he is able to forgive Ruby's deception and show a more mellow side, as he asks to be "parrrdoned" for his actions.

"Gordon, the old sea captain, and his sidekick, Crab Davey, provide a lot of comedic relief."
—Mike Murray,
Supervising
Technical Director

1–8: Guillermo "Willie" Real •
9: William Salazar • 10: Timothy Lamb

106

Gordon & Doug Concepts

① ② ③

7

8

9

10

DAVEY

1

2

3

"In one way, Gordon represents what the human world, what we as people who don't know the Gillmans, might think of krakens, as these big monsters. He's Ahab searching for his Moby Dick; he's really the one who sees them as monsters and profits a little bit off them. I think the decision to make him as unhinged but as goofy as possible gives us a lot of comedy. We needed a character like Gordon, because there's an aspect of exposure—of being seen as what you fear you are—that we needed Ruby to feel. We did need an outside character who maybe sees the worst of her first. And I know that Gordon is a very heightened character, but I think we do have moments where he really represents, hopefully, how the audience will feel: 'Oh, now I look at krakens in a different way.'"
—FARYN PEARL, CO-DIRECTOR

1, 6: Alexandre Puvilland • 2: production model: Hannah Kang • 3: concept model: Charles Ellison • 4: Anthony Holden • 5, 8, 9: Pierre-Olivier Vincent • 7: production render: Jaewon Lee; surfacing: Sara V. Cembalisty

GORDON'S TOUR BUS
MONSTERS ARE REAL!

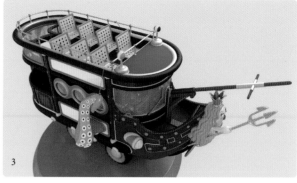

1–3, 8, 9: PRODUCTION MODEL: PAUL SCHOENI • 4: PIERRE-OLIVIER VINCENT • 5: CONCEPT MODEL: PIERRE-OLIVIER VINCENT • 6: DRAWOVER: PIERRE-OLIVIER VINCENT • 7, 11–13: FREDERIC WILLIAM STEWART • 10: PRODUCTION MODEL: PAUL SCHOENI; SURFACING: JEREMY ENGLEMAN

"There's one person who opposes them, one person who threatens to expose them for the sea creatures that they are, and that is Gordon. He is antagonistic from the very beginning, and we get a sense right there that, 'Oh, watch out for that guy.' Ruby knows it, we know it, and we feel that. He serves as a bit of a red herring to make us feel like not all is perfect, not all is safe, so that when she goes forward and has a big change and becomes a kraken, not only does Gordon start sniffing her out, but now the whole town is on high alert: 'Oh, there's something that destroyed the library, and it's loose, and it could come back, and it could destroy us now.'"
—GLENN HARMON, HEAD OF STORY

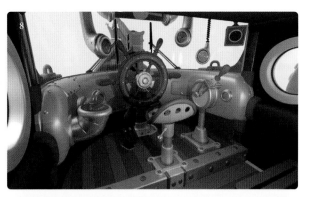

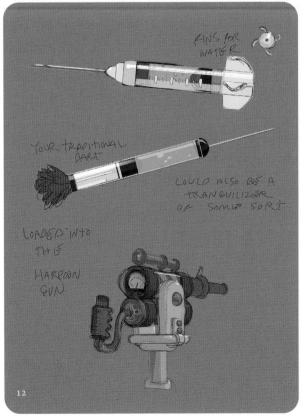

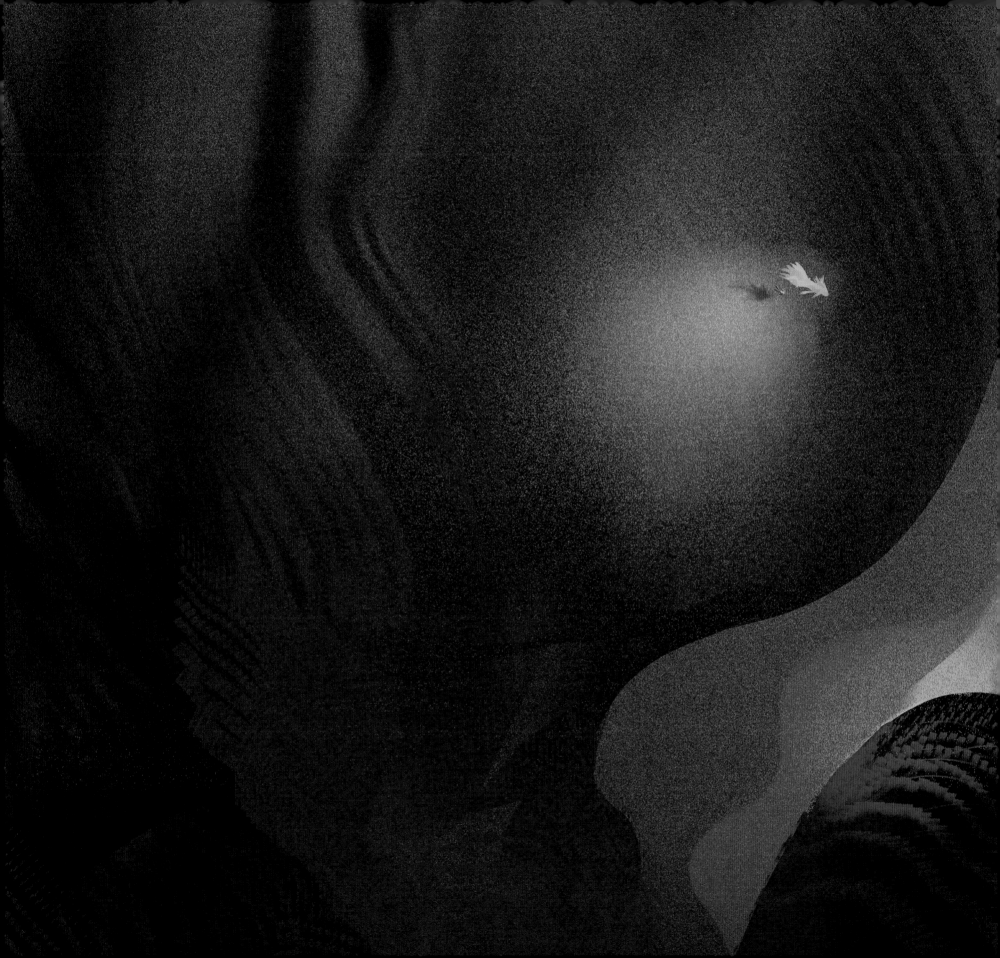

Part 2
Sea

Kraken Ruby

Ruby is possibly the most powerful kraken in the history of mythic monsters. Stronger than Scylla and as confident as Charybdis, she is not a monster to be messed with. Of course, this all comes later after being kept in the dark about her true nature by her family, emboldened by her grandmother (a kraken queen!), and betrayed by a high school BFF (Best Fiend Forever!) who turns out to be a mermaid—and a particularly poisonous one, at that. Ruby has had to learn an awful lot about her kraken heritage and try to master her latent powers in a short span of time. It turns out that she's a natural. Her youthful humility means she won't turn out like Grandmamah and succumb to pride, and her earnestness means she hasn't yet learned to dissimulate like her mother. Ruby's pure heart powers her kraken potential, and the undersea criminal element is already quaking!

PREVIOUS SPREAD: FREDERIC WILLIAM STEWART • 1, 6: JULIEN LE ROLLAND • 2–5, 7: TIMOTHY LAMB

EMPOWERED BY HER NEWFOUND STRENGTH + SIZE!

...BUT STILL AN INSECURE TEEN

1

2

3

SCALE!

4

5

"You have to space out the storyboards; you have to have a good knowledge of film scores and music that you put in temporarily or decide not to use any music at that particular point, and you have to know when to let the moment breathe and ask for additional boards if needed. That's one nice thing—as the editor on animated films, you can request something from the story department or the animation department, and you'll get it the next day, which is amazing."
—MICHELLE MENDENHALL, LEAD EDITOR

6

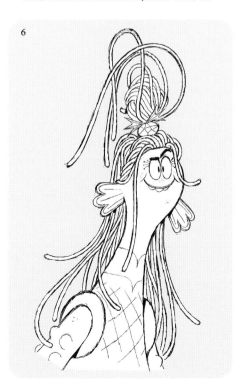

7

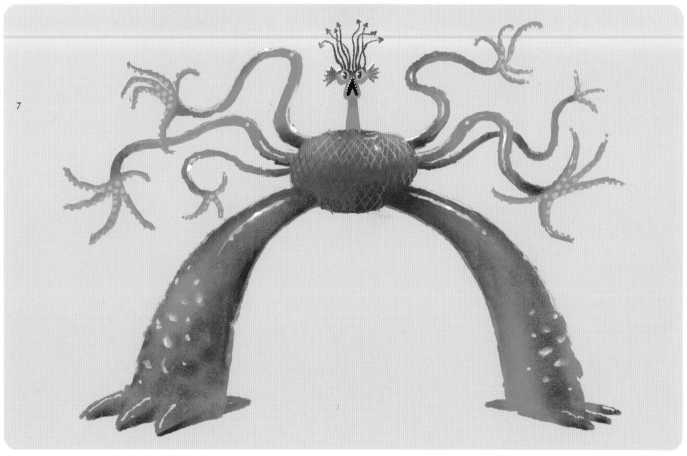

THIS SPREAD: TIMOTHY LAMB

"I think one of the things that's interesting for me about the giant character design is that POV really wanted them to have an internal structure, so they've got bones inside them, they've got cells, and they've got some scales on top. They've got all this extra detail that must work together, and we've never done anything at DreamWorks where we build an internal structure for characters, as far as I know. Giant Ruby is built very physically, so everything about her is designed as it would be in the real world, which helps us do things like simulate light more effectively. There was a lot of, 'Okay, if we were building this, how would we build it in real life?' And then there is an awful lot of, 'Okay, how do we handle the complexity of it so that what is animated is a much more stripped-down version of the character—the least bits possible?'"
—DAVE WALVOORD,
VFX SUPERVISOR

THIS SPREAD: TIMOTHY LAMB

118

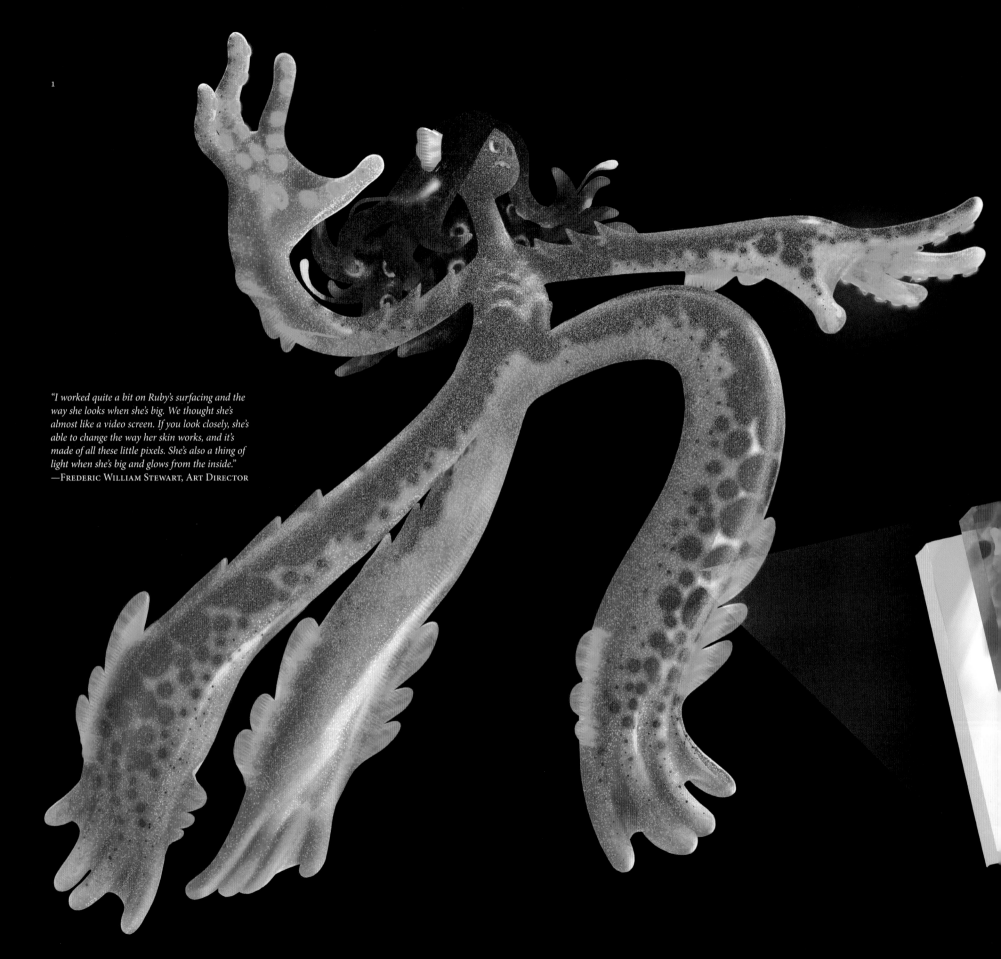

"I worked quite a bit on Ruby's surfacing and the way she looks when she's big. We thought she's almost like a video screen. If you look closely, she's able to change the way her skin works, and it's made of all these little pixels. She's also a thing of light when she's big and glows from the inside."
—FREDERIC WILLIAM STEWART, ART DIRECTOR

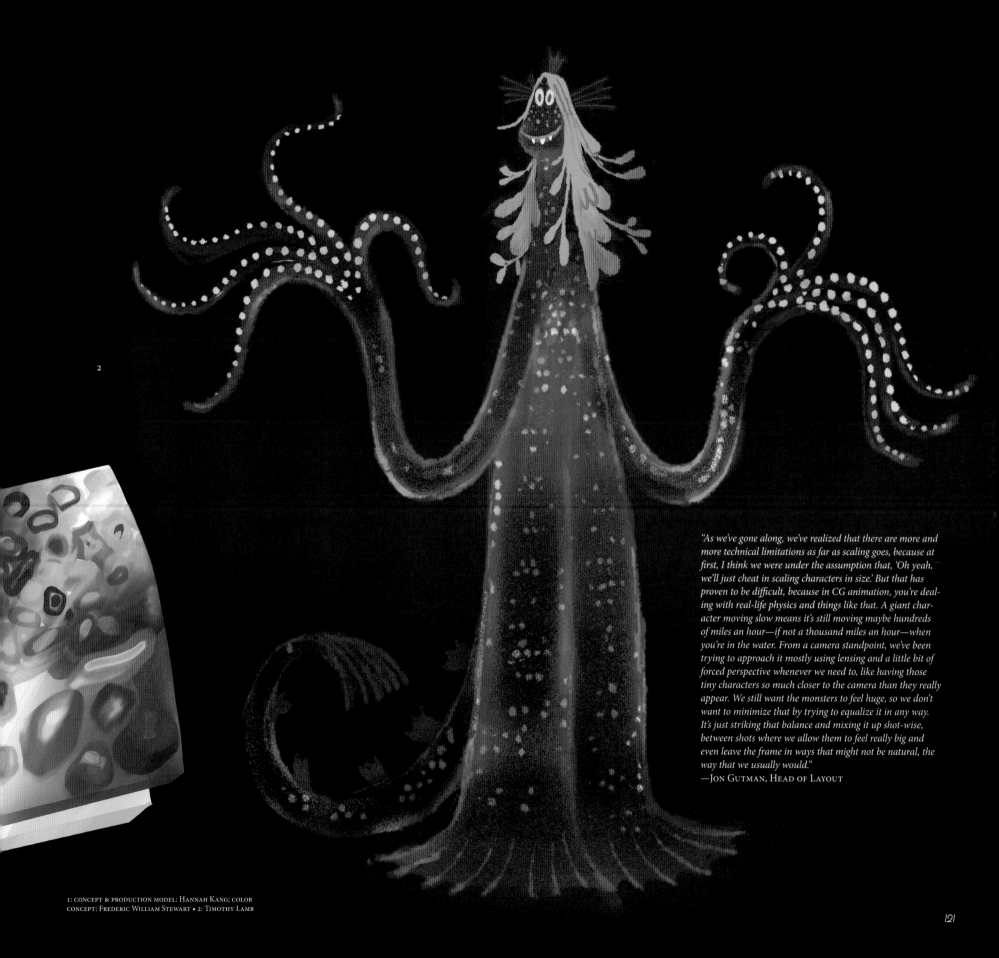

"As we've gone along, we've realized that there are more and more technical limitations as far as scaling goes, because at first, I think we were under the assumption that, 'Oh yeah, we'll just cheat in scaling characters in size.' But that has proven to be difficult, because in CG animation, you're dealing with real-life physics and things like that. A giant character moving slow means it's still moving maybe hundreds of miles an hour—if not a thousand miles an hour—when you're in the water. From a camera standpoint, we've been trying to approach it mostly using lensing and a little bit of forced perspective whenever we need to, like having those tiny characters so much closer to the camera than they really appear. We still want the monsters to feel huge, so we don't want to minimize that by trying to equalize it in any way. It's just striking that balance and mixing it up shot-wise, between shots where we allow them to feel really big and even leave the frame in ways that might not be natural, the way that we usually would."
—Jon Gutman, Head of Layout

1: CONCEPT & PRODUCTION MODEL: HANNAH KANG; COLOR
CONCEPT: FREDERIC WILLIAM STEWART • 2: TIMOTHY LAMB

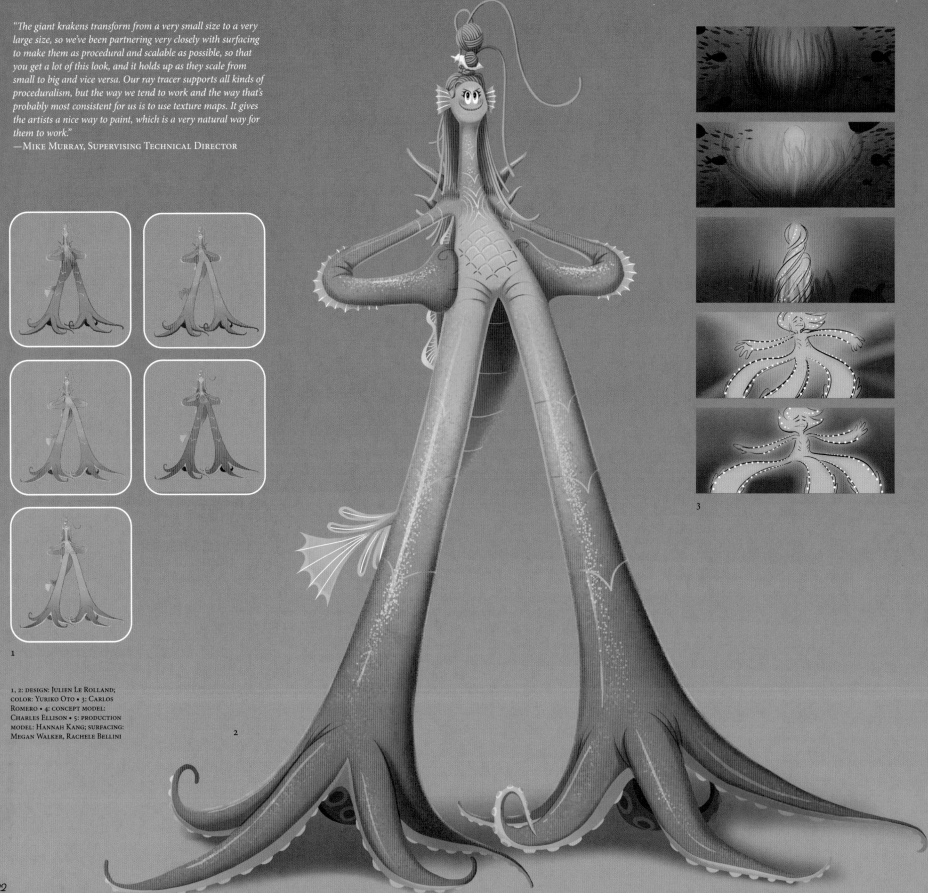

"The giant krakens transform from a very small size to a very large size, so we've been partnering very closely with surfacing to make them as procedural and scalable as possible, so that you get a lot of this look, and it holds up as they scale from small to big and vice versa. Our ray tracer supports all kinds of proceduralism, but the way we tend to work and the way that's probably most consistent for us is to use texture maps. It gives the artists a nice way to paint, which is a very natural way for them to work."
—MIKE MURRAY, SUPERVISING TECHNICAL DIRECTOR

1

2

3

1, 2: DESIGN: JULIEN LE ROLLAND; COLOR: YURIKO OTO • 3: CARLOS ROMERO • 4: CONCEPT MODEL: CHARLES ELLISON • 5: PRODUCTION MODEL: HANNAH KANG; SURFACING: MEGAN WALKER, RACHELE BELLINI

default   bioluminescent   activated

Kraken Agatha

Agatha finally becomes her warrior kraken self when the threat to her family and way of life are threatened by the titan Nerissa. Boasting four massive legs, Agatha is surprisingly nimble for such a huge monster and has mastered many of the marine martial arts. Krakens tend not to use handheld weapons, as their entire bodies are weaponized. Agatha can shoot pulsed-energy blasts and can rely on her wits and fearlessness to counter any threat. Although rusty (real estate calls for a different type of warfare), she proves her mettle in the climactic fight and although badly hurt, she joins Ruby in defeating the titan.

1–3, 7: Guillermo "Willie" Real •
4–6, 8: Timothy Lamb

124

Mega Agatha
Concepts

7

8

2

3

4

"For the krakens, we had to figure out what amount of internal glow looks good, based on what environment they're in and how much of their glow interacts with their surroundings. For instance, if their hand passes by a building, does the building light up when the hand passes? There is an issue with depth. When you have things that are translucent, we have to keep an eye out for that. So when something is small and has a translucent material, it will be bright because the idea is that the light goes through it. If it's smaller, it'll scatter more light, but for the giants, they're tricky because they're super-big, so we must make sure that they don't end up looking miniature based on how much translucency and scattering they have."
—JOANNA WU, HEAD OF LIGHTING

1: JULIEN LE ROLLAND • 2, 3: CONCEPT MODEL: CHARLES ELLISON; HAIR DRAWOVER: PIERRE-OLIVIER VINCENT • 4: CONCEPT MODEL: CHARLES ELLISON

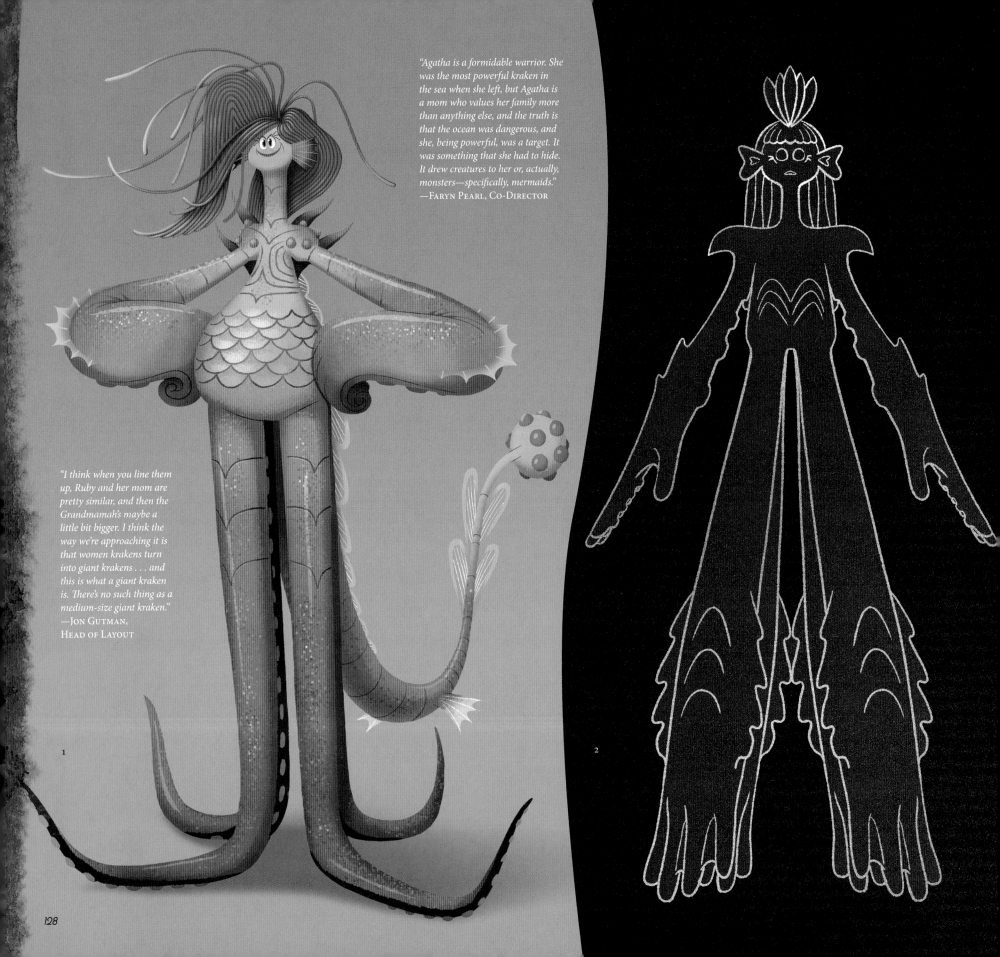

"Agatha is a formidable warrior. She was the most powerful kraken in the sea when she left, but Agatha is a mom who values her family more than anything else, and the truth is that the ocean was dangerous, and she, being powerful, was a target. It was something that she had to hide. It drew creatures to her or, actually, monsters—specifically, mermaids."
—Faryn Pearl, Co-Director

"I think when you line them up, Ruby and her mom are pretty similar, and then the Grandmamah's maybe a little bit bigger. I think the way we're approaching it is that women krakens turn into giant krakens . . . and this is what a giant kraken is. There's no such thing as a medium-size giant kraken."
—Jon Gutman, Head of Layout

1

2

"With Agatha, you're trying to get maximum contrast from her business life and her daughter. Ruby has only ever known her mother as a very button-down-clad, power-suit-wearing, real-estate saleswoman who's all about the rules. When she turns into a giant kraken, it was kind of like, 'Oh man. Bright pink on red with stripes.' The pitch was, 'It's like seeing pictures of your mom in the '70s.'"
—Frederic William Stewart, Art Director

1: design: Julien Le Rolland; color: Yuriko Oto • 2, 4: Pierre-Olivier Vincent • 3: concept
& production model: Catherin Cubillan Reyes; color concept: Frederic William Stewart

3

4

Grandmamah

Well-armed or legged, the kraken queen (voiced by Jane Fonda) is very much large and in charge. She has reigned over the underwater world for many years and is ready to pass on the scepter. Somewhat dismayed by Agatha's refusal to take up her responsibility and rather annoyed by Brill's feeble-mindedness, she has her hopes set on her granddaughter. She can barely contain her glee when Ruby's inadvertent dip in the ocean broadcasts the news that there is a new giant kraken. It quickens her pulse! She cleverly baits the hook for Ruby but doesn't understand that young Ruby is made of sterner stuff and even-keeled—she really wants to be on that boat for prom, so undersea kingdoms can wait. In the end, Grandmamah realizes that with the third generation, there's a third way.

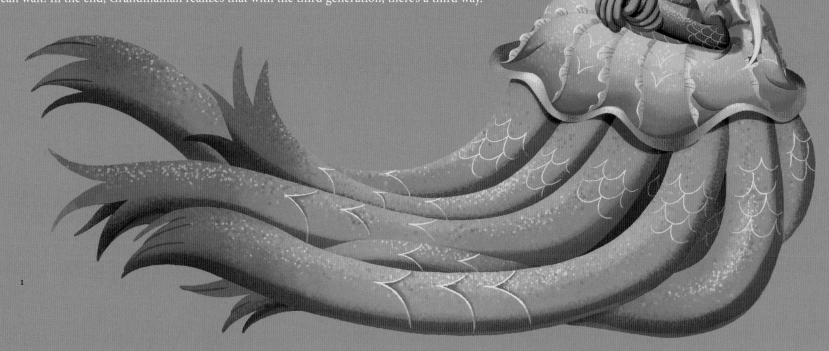

1

2

3

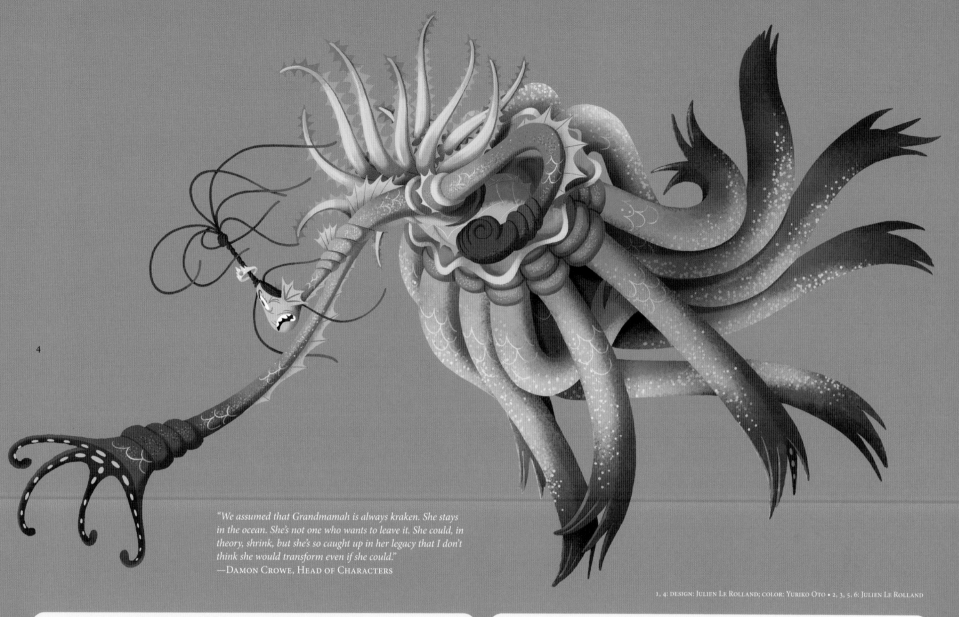

"We assumed that Grandmamah is always kraken. She stays in the ocean. She's not one who wants to leave it. She could, in theory, shrink, but she's so caught up in her legacy that I don't think she would transform even if she could."
—Damon Crowe, Head of Characters

1, 4: design: Julien Le Rolland; color: Yuriko Oto • 2, 3, 5, 6: Julien Le Rolland

ORTOPEDIC LIMB IN THE TRADITION OF DREAMWORKS

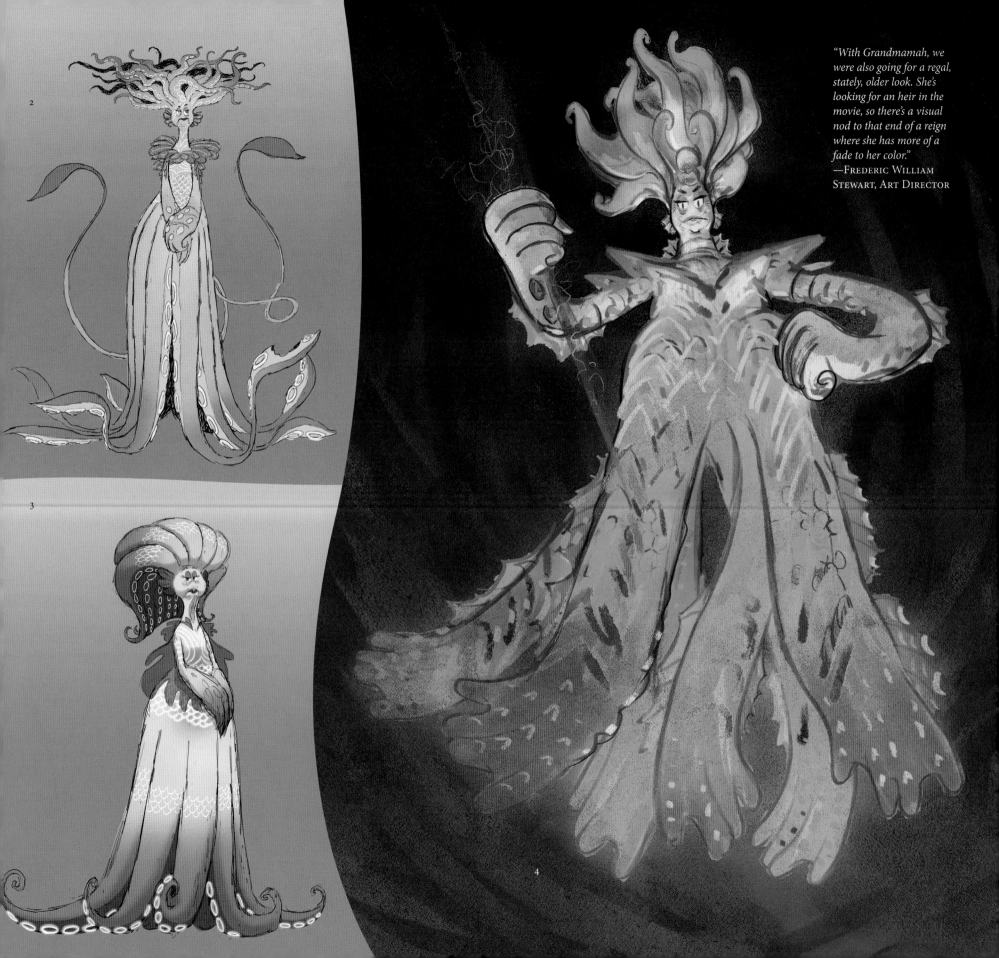

2

3

4

"With Grandmamah, we were also going for a regal, stately, older look. She's looking for an heir in the movie, so there's a visual nod to that end of a reign where she has more of a fade to her color."
—Frederic William Stewart, Art Director

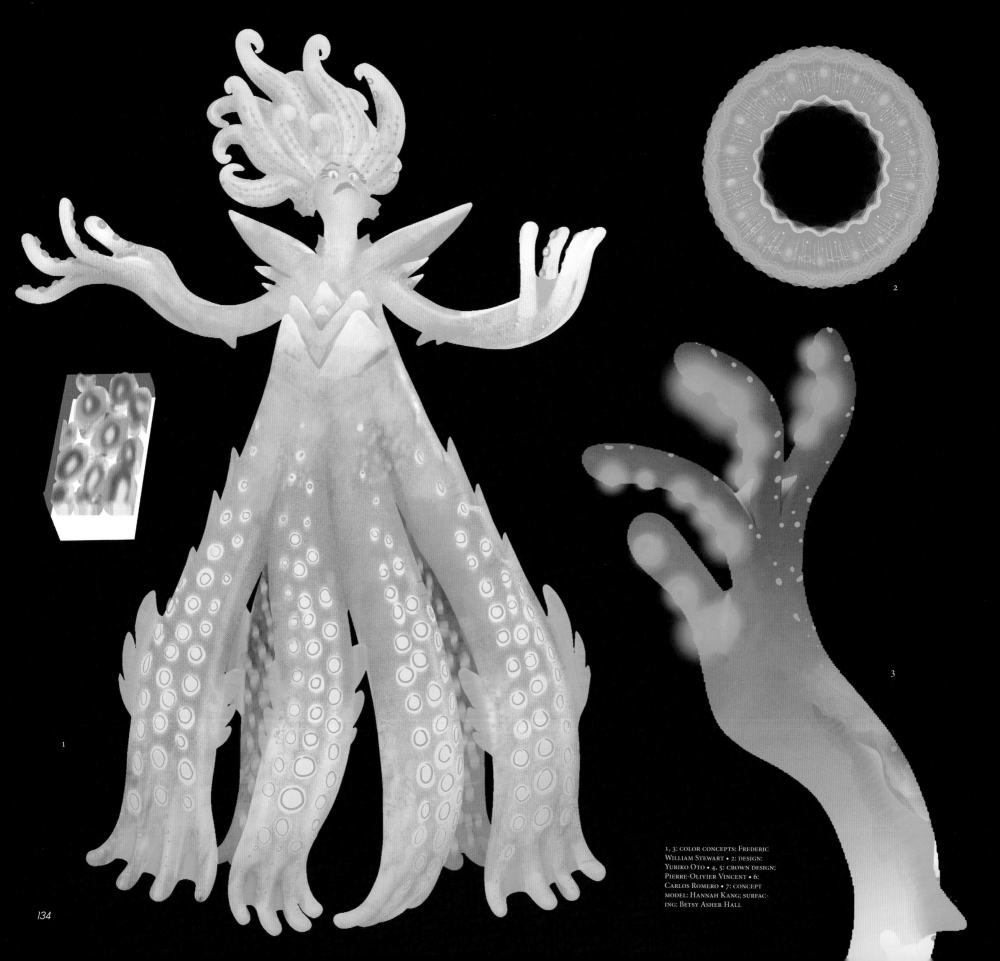

134

1, 3: COLOR CONCEPTS: FREDERIC
WILLIAM STEWART • 2: DESIGN:
YURIKO OTO • 4, 5: CROWN DESIGN:
PIERRE-OLIVIER VINCENT • 6:
CARLOS ROMERO • 7: CONCEPT
MODEL: HANNAH KANG; SURFAC-
ING: BETSY ASHER HALL

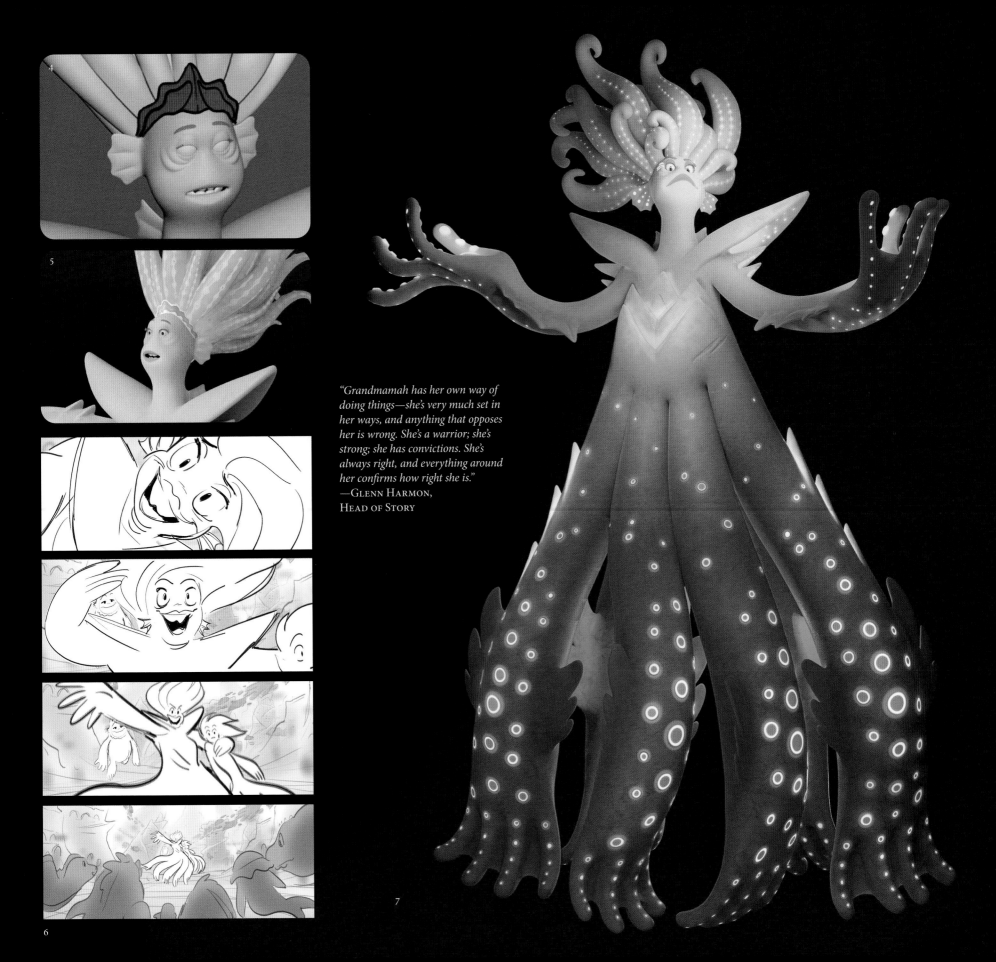

"Grandmamah has her own way of doing things—she's very much set in her ways, and anything that opposes her is wrong. She's a warrior; she's strong; she has convictions. She's always right, and everything around her confirms how right she is."
—Glenn Harmon,
Head of Story

Titan Nerissa

Finally, the scales fall off Ruby's eyes, and Chelsea is revealed to be the titan Nerissa, the mermaid queen, clothed in red, forbidding scales, hair of water, and a fearsome visage. Biding her time after being defeated by kraken Agatha, she has waited many years until she could target the innocent and naive teenage Ruby. Pretending to befriend her and preying on her insecurities, Nerissa could barely conceal her glee in seeing Ruby succeed in obtaining the powerful Trident of Oceanus, and then when handed it, why, what great joy in knowing she had the krakens right where she wanted them. Her plan had been "trident and tested," and now comes the coup de grâce. She'll try to kill the kraken aristocracy and Oceanside in one swell blow.

1

"*Titan Nerissa is a person on top and a fish on the bottom, but she's scaled all over, and the scales are almost black. Hers are almost inverted, really putting focus on the scalloped edge rather than the round edge. She's really dark, and then her hair, which is kind of a magical thing, is glowing—so she almost always comes out as a silhouette, where the light of her hair behind her puts her dark scales in contrast.*"
—Frederic William Stewart, Art Director

2

"*Who would be the most vicious enemy to what you think would be the most vicious creature in the sea? So of course, we chose the most benign, the most beloved: the mermaids. It's a great, classic DreamWorks twist. Nerissa can be seductive. She does say what Ruby wants to hear, and what Ruby wants to hear is very sweet: she wants to have someone that she could be her whole self with, who she doesn't have to hide from. But Nerissa lures Ruby in and, once Ruby is completely on her side, takes the trident for her own evil ends.*"
—Faryn Pearl, Co-Director

1, 2, 4, 5: Taylor Krahenbuhl
• 3: Ryan Savas

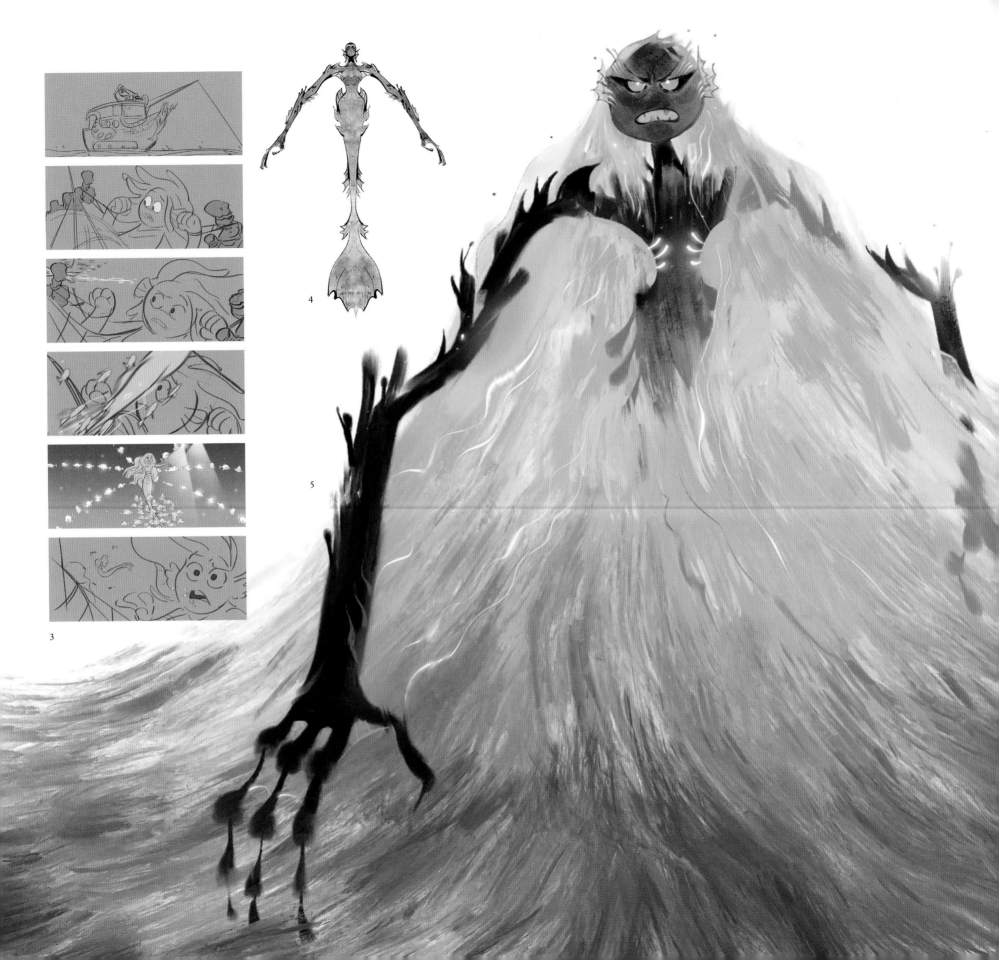

3

4

5

"The titan mermaid's hair is made of water, and I think we have a good look for it, and we have a good idea how to integrate it with a simulation of the water on the ocean surface. But we want to make sure it can handle some additional moves. She's going to be big, moving around; we want to make sure that's working. You want to make sure she feels big. That's one thing we're asking our animators to do: don't animate her like she's human-size, because then when she swings around, everything's going to be supersonic. We deal a lot with the scale of things, especially for water. Everyone knows what it looks like. If you do something a little bit off, people are going to pick up on it, and you must make it believable even in a fantastic environment."
—Lawrence Lee, Head of VFX

4

"Once underwater, the hair has got to move, but we must make it believable when the currents are affecting it. But so it doesn't become distracting, we also do some fluid dynamics a lot of times . . . so it's running another level of simulation before we even run the hair simulation. We'll put an artificial tank of particles around the character and give that a little bit of motion behavior in it, and then transfer that onto the hair, or let the hair simulate inside that tank of effects. We'll also do some simpler tricks, which are more like giving the simulation a generic, almost sine wave–like behavior to it, like a mathematical kind of application, and then let the simulation take that and make it a lot more organic."
—CHRISTOPHER MICHAEL, CFX SUPERVISOR

Marine Life

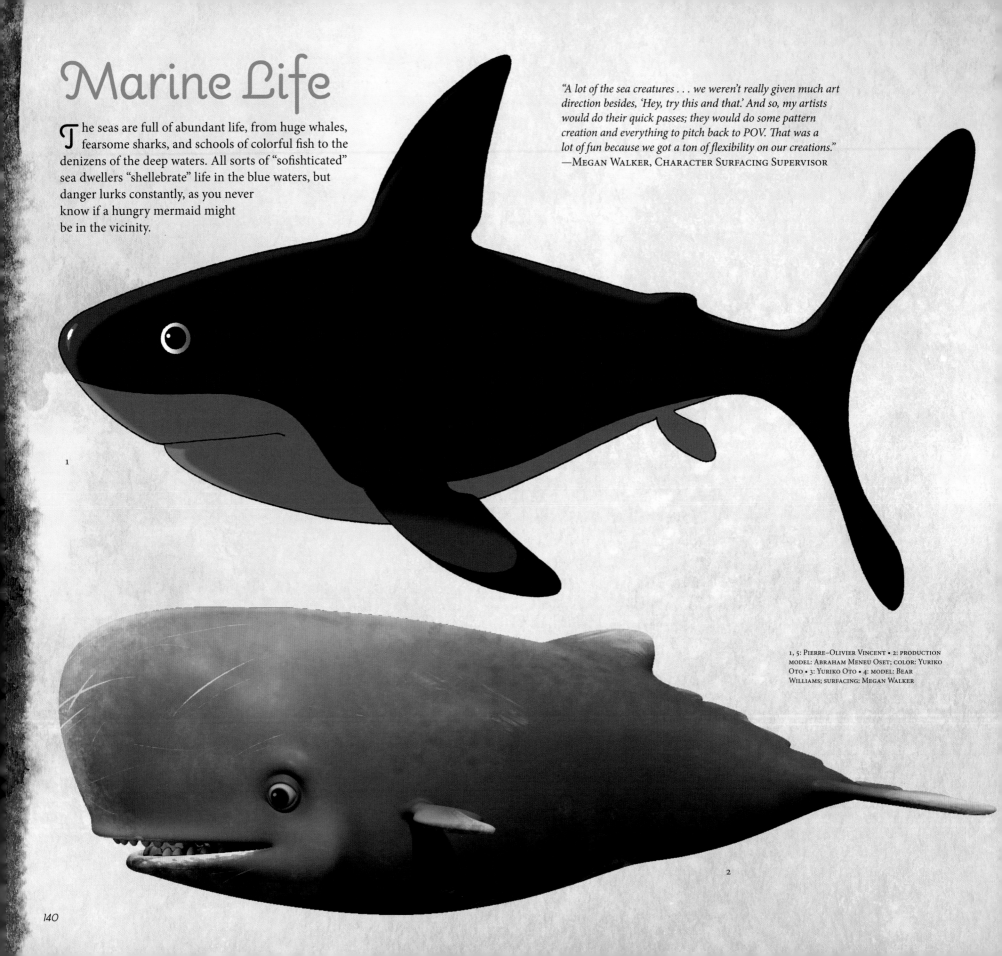

The seas are full of abundant life, from huge whales, fearsome sharks, and schools of colorful fish to the denizens of the deep waters. All sorts of "sofishticated" sea dwellers "shellebrate" life in the blue waters, but danger lurks constantly, as you never know if a hungry mermaid might be in the vicinity.

"A lot of the sea creatures . . . we weren't really given much art direction besides, 'Hey, try this and that.' And so, my artists would do their quick passes; they would do some pattern creation and everything to pitch back to POV. That was a lot of fun because we got a ton of flexibility on our creations."
—Megan Walker, Character Surfacing Supervisor

1

1, 5: Pierre–Olivier Vincent • 2: production model: Abraham Meneu Oset; color: Yuriko Oto • 3: Yuriko Oto • 4: model: Bear Williams; surfacing: Megan Walker

2

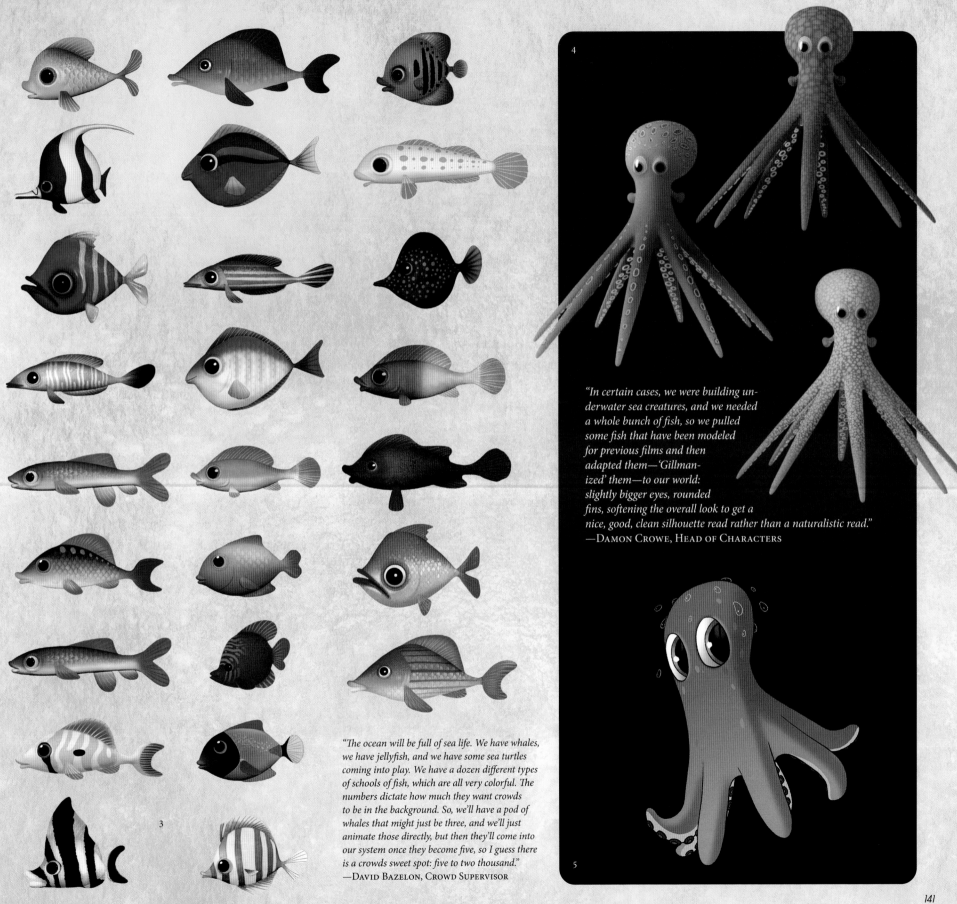

"In certain cases, we were building underwater sea creatures, and we needed a whole bunch of fish, so we pulled some fish that have been modeled for previous films and then adapted them—'Gillmanized' them—to our world: slightly bigger eyes, rounded fins, softening the overall look to get a nice, good, clean silhouette read rather than a naturalistic read."
—DAMON CROWE, HEAD OF CHARACTERS

"The ocean will be full of sea life. We have whales, we have jellyfish, and we have some sea turtles coming into play. We have a dozen different types of schools of fish, which are all very colorful. The numbers dictate how much they want crowds to be in the background. So, we'll have a pod of whales that might just be three, and we'll just animate those directly, but then they'll come into our system once they become five, so I guess there is a crowds sweet spot: five to two thousand."
—DAVID BAZELON, CROWD SUPERVISOR

The Reef

On her journey to the kraken palace, Ruby first navigates the reef, a place of sunlit waters and abundant forests of kelp. As the seaweed slowly drifts in the current, Ruby has plenty of time to ponder her current status as new kraken on the block.

1–5: Yuriko Oto • 6: Pierre–Olivier Vincent

1

2

"POV loves detail—an extreme amount of detail—and it's a little bit of a running joke with our team. Our main set-dresser is now the kelp specialist because there are hundreds and thousands of individually set-dressed kelp that are placed specifically around the performance of her animation, and of course, as we set-dress, POV jokes, 'More, more, more; more is more; we want more.' Downstream department CFX is having to sim all the kelp underwater, so the more we put in there, the more they must do their work, and the more rendering time it takes."
—David Valera, Final Layout Supervisor

"The kelp forest appears in two different sequences in the film, and they are massive. There are hundreds of individual kelp plants, so we've been working on those, and they take a lot of investment, but it really does transport you into this awesome underwater kingdom. When Ruby first transforms in the ocean, this kelp envelops her, and it really is like, 'Oh man, this is a little creepy.'"
—Christopher Michael, CFX Supervisor

3

4

5

The Canyon

Just before the ocean floor lies a foreboding canyon. There is no light, save the ripples of sea currents. Out of the darkness loom towering rock formations. It's a truly desolate place. Will Ruby be frightened by the "fishure" and turn back? No! She gorges on the adventurous feelings and keeps going, her uncle still ahead of her and her new kraken powers lighting the way. It may be gloomy and unsettling, but it's a grand canyon, nonetheless.

1, 2: PRODUCTION RENDER MODEL: KULL SHIN (SEUNG YOUB); SURFACING: SARA V. CEMBALISTY • 3, 4 & OVERLEAF: FREDERIC WILLIAM STEWART

"With the undersea canyons, it doesn't ever go to black, so when there's nothing there, it's trickier for us, because then we still have to create interest out of nothingness. For something like that, you would get monochromatic lighting, and if there's stuff there, it's easier. If they do set-dress big blocks of things, even if there's no surfacing on it, there will be some dim silhouette. If there isn't, then we must create interest out of nowhere, so a lot of times, we may create our own gradients, or we can drop in little particles to give visual interest. Sometimes we'll create 'God rays,' so that will give you shape and an interest that's not given to us by another department, so when there's nothing there, it is harder. But I think sometimes it's more fun, and sometimes you're just frustrated because we have those empty frames."
—JOANNA WU, HEAD OF LIGHTING

4

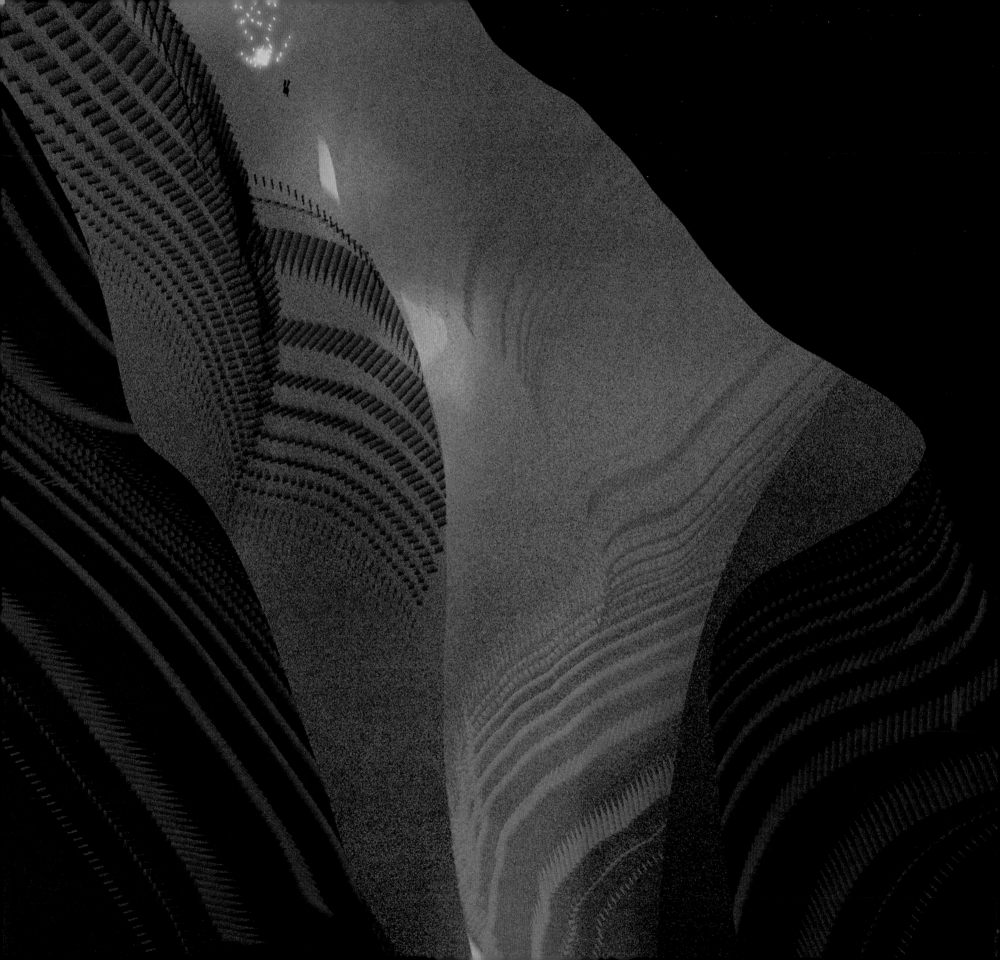

The Palace

1–3: PRODUCTION MODEL: EMILIE AUSTIN, KULL SHIN (SEUNG YOUB); SURFACING: SARA V. CEMBALISTY •
4, 5: PIERRE–OLIVIER VINCENT

Coming into view on the ocean floor, the kraken palace is quite a sight. Here the kraken queen resides (alas, no Prince of Whales) and governs over all other undersea kingdoms. Inside the palace there are many rooms, including the throne room where Ruby will meet her grandmother for the first time. Vast murals depicting kraken history decorate the palace, while visiting dignitaries wait to commune with the great queen. The palace is testimony to the size and power of the krakens. No expense has been spared in decorating it, from squid-glass chandeliers to jewel-encrusted towers and gigantic statues. Ruby's now a kraken princess, but will she get the "whalecome"
she deserves?

4

1–4: Pierre–Olivier Vincent • 5, 6: production render models: Erin Caswell; surfacing: Woojin Choi • 7: production shot render

"When you look at the kraken castle, you wouldn't have to stretch very far to imagine that this castle is suddenly moving into the landscape to go to another location."
—PIERRE-OLIVIER VINCENT, PRODUCTION DESIGNER

1–8: PIERRE–OLIVIER VINCENT

1

2

3

4

"The castle is very textural, but there's a lot of curves. There are no straight lines, and when you go inside the kraken castle, the thought process was: we know it's a very luxurious environment. It's obviously a place of power. You have the grandmother in there, ruling her people, but also controlling some part of the ocean. Every time you think about those big powers, even on our Earth, you think about luxurious materials, such as gold and beautiful woodwork, and I wanted to try to find a way to represent this. I used a lot of materials that would have, in a way, a sort of watery quality, like glass and jade—materials that would have a certain softness just because of the way the light is going through them, but at the same time, bringing a patina to it. So, it's an ancient power, but we didn't want to make it so old-looking that when Ruby is joining the kraken world, she couldn't picture herself eventually living there."
—Pierre-Olivier Vincent, Production Designer

5

6

7

8

153

1

2

3

4

5

6

"At the bottom of the ocean floor, we set-dressed a bunch of stalagmite columns to give the kraken castle a bit of scale, but everything falls off into deep, dark nothingness from the midground to the background. As we get into the kraken castle itself and the throne room . . . POV designed a lot of these very intricate globes and spheres that have individual pieces that are rotating, which look like these sorts of spiral sculptures. We animated a lot of the noncharacter assets in the movie. The throne room has these wavy walls that are individual assets, spinning at different rates and different speeds against each other, so there's always something in the environment that feels relatively alive. There's always something going on, as well as when we get into the murals and the hall, when Grandmamah was telling Ruby about the history of the krakens versus all the other sea creatures, especially the mermaids. Those are individual assets that we broke apart, and it's a collaboration between our team and Carlos Fernandez Puertolas's team to animate them."
—David Valera,
Final Layout Supervisor

7

"When you see Grandmamah's castle, everything's made from these beautiful minerals and stones. The surfacing department did a wild job on it. It looks so rich and ornate but is still appealing and colorful."
—Faryn Pearl, Co-Director

1: production model: Kull Shin (Seung youb); surfacing: Woojin Choi • 2: production model: Angela Arzumanyan; surfacing: Woojin Choi • 3, 5: production model: Bear Williams; surfacing: Woojin Choi • 4: production model: Emilie Austin; surfacing: Woojin Choi • 6, 7: production model: Hannah Kang; surfacing: Sara V. Cembalisty

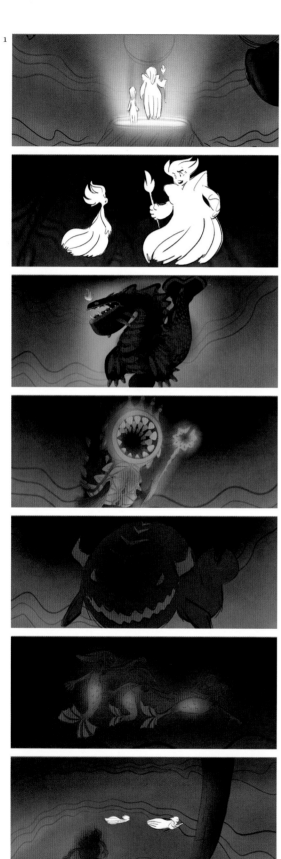

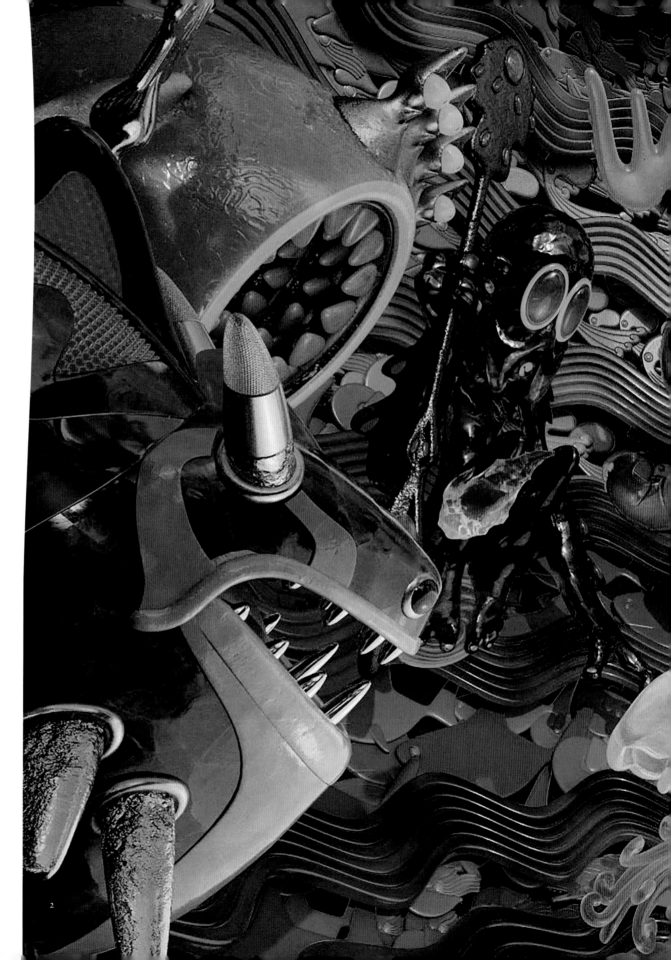

1: Carlos Romero • 2: production model: Jaewon Lee,
Erin Caswell, Bear Williams, Emilie Austin, Hannah
Kang, Kull Shin (Seung youb), Angela Arzumanyan

156

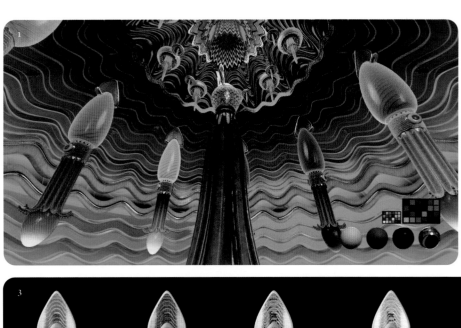

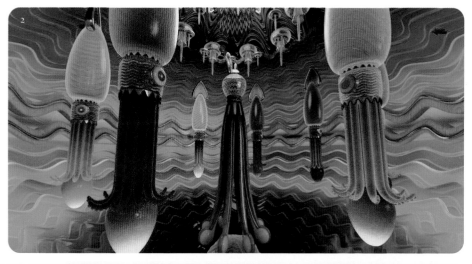

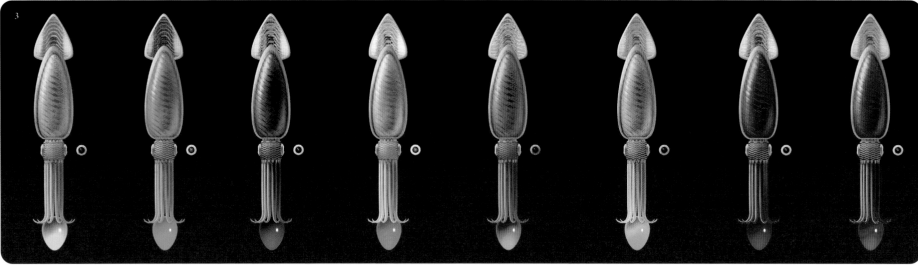

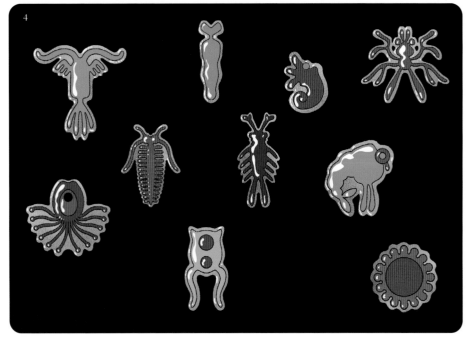

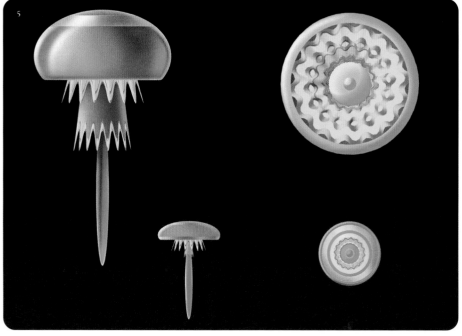

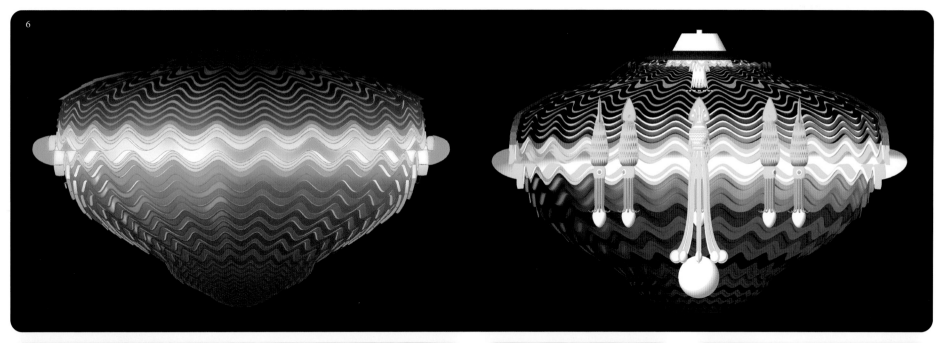

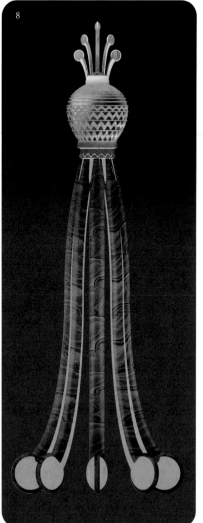

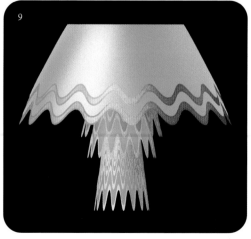

"I work with the directors daily, and the script is always evolving, and we've had a few different writers as we go. The writing is constantly changing; the script is constantly changing. An animated movie is always evolving, and something that maybe was working one week . . . when you're working on some other part, you realize, 'Oh, this is going to be better if we change something in the beginning.'"
—MICHELLE MENDENHALL, LEAD EDITOR

1, 2: PRODUCTION MODEL: ANGELA ARZUMANYAN; SURFACING: WOOJIN CHOI • 3–9: CONCEPT DESIGNS: PIERRE-OLIVIER VINCENT • OVERLEAF: FREDERIC WILLIAM STEWART

The Well of Seas

The source of the world's sea currents is a massive underwater volcano, and to get near it, one must really go with the flow. That's a lot trickier in practice, however, and Ruby must train hard to break through the currents if she is to have a chance to grab the Trident of Oceanus hidden within the forbidding caldera. If she can succeed, she'll graduate "magma-cum-laude," but then, alas, Chelsea will show her true credentials with a "master's" in betrayal.

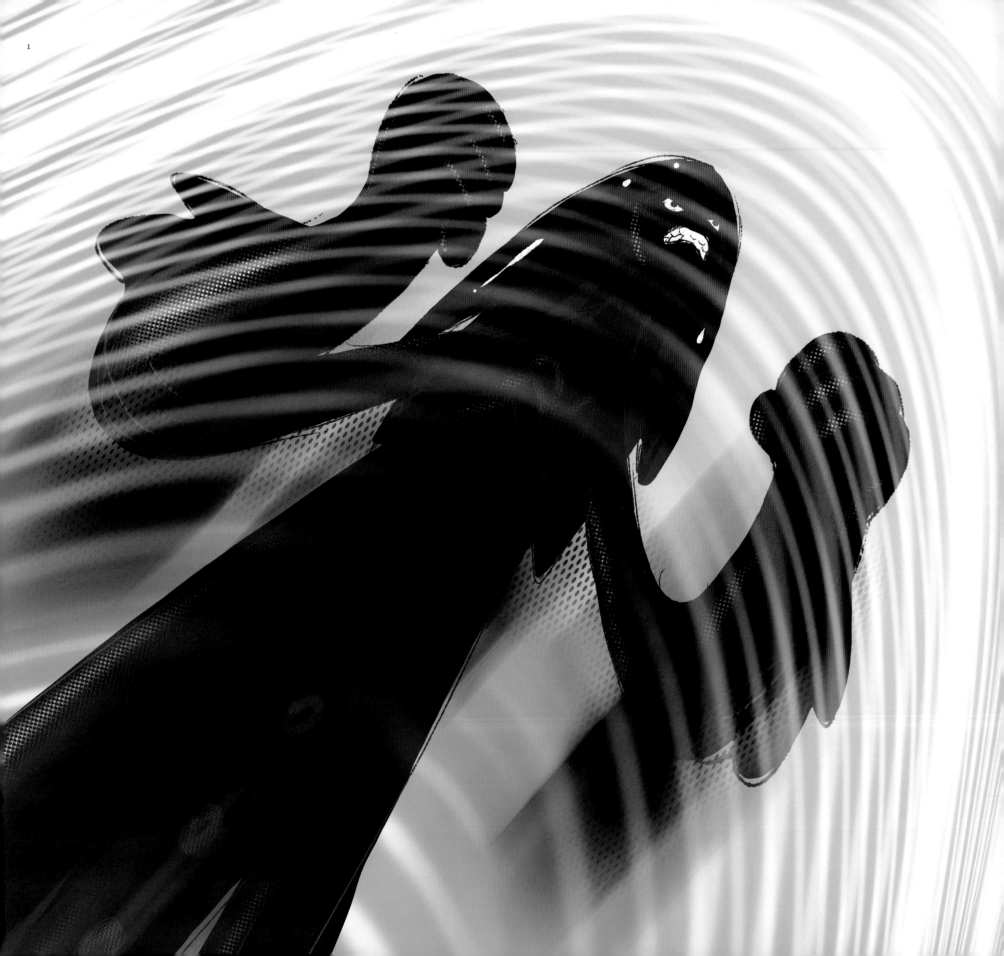

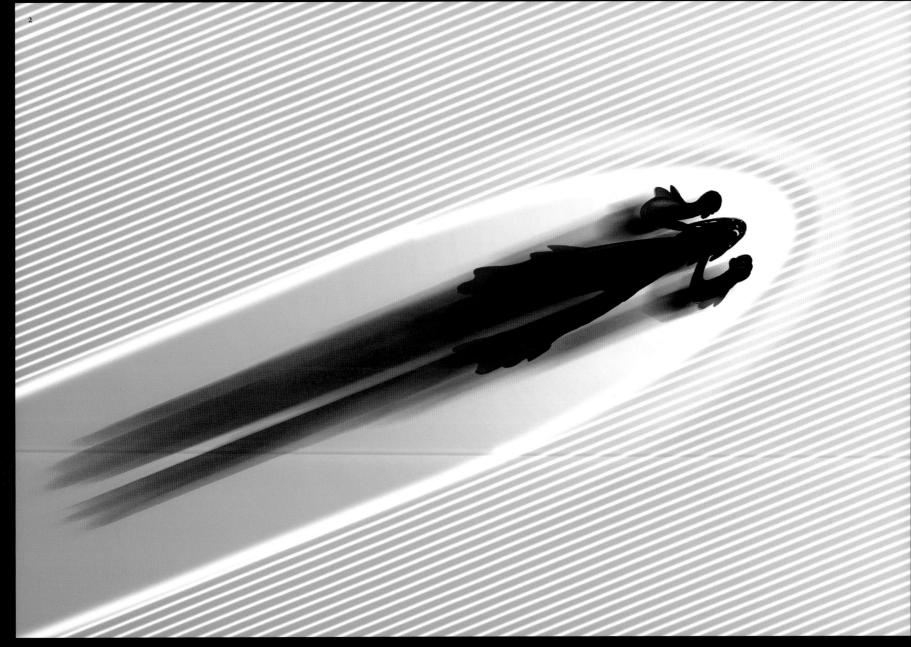

"The Well of Seas stuff that POV and Fred did—that's something that was entirely conceived by them. I think POV's amazing at realizing these fantastic worlds, and I think he was feeling like we need something at that point in the movie that's really going to make it clear that this is not the underwater world that we're familiar with. When we first saw the art for that stuff, I was like, 'It's going to be amazing.'"
—JON GUTMAN, HEAD OF LAYOUT

"One thing we always try to impart on our partners in our departments is motion and scale, and when something is big, we want them to be slow and lumbering, because then the FX elements supporting it will feel right in terms of scale. It's a big deal, because later in the movie we have an underwater magnetic volcano . . . it's huge. The opening of the caldera is possibly a mile and half across. There's a sphere in there that's almost half a mile wide, which is hiding the trident that Ruby's got to enter and grab. If you put that next to Ruby, Ruby's just a dot."
—LAWRENCE LEE, HEAD OF VFX

"The underwater kingdom has its own style, and what stands out to me is how massive, how huge it is . . . it's endless. POV directed the teams to create these swirled grooves and horizontal fluting that goes throughout the ground of it. But it does still have direction that takes you to the castle. I think there are a couple of things at play. We go to this volcanic area, so I think POV wanted to capitalize on that—the underground is very much sculpted by the volcanic folding and moving and pushing and nudging, which gives you these curves. Sometimes POV would pull us back in and say, 'You know, you're thinking too logically about that. We just want this beautiful. We need the look. We need the flow.' He would say that quite often. 'It creates a flow.'"
—JASON TURNER, HEAD OF LOCATIONS

1

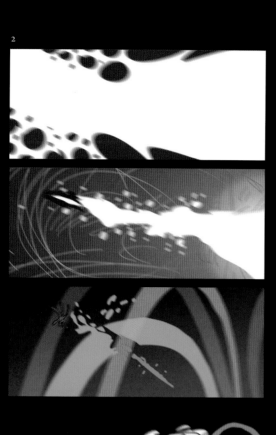

2

3

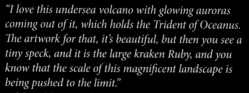

4

5

"I love this undersea volcano with glowing auroras coming out of it, which holds the Trident of Oceanus. The artwork for that, it's beautiful, but then you see a tiny speck, and it is the large kraken Ruby, and you know that the scale of this magnificent landscape is being pushed to the limit."
—MIKE MURRAY, SUPERVISING TECHNICAL DIRECTOR

1: FREDERIC WILLIAM STEWART • 2: DAVE WOLTER • 3–5: PRELIMINARY
F/X WORK: DEREK CHEUNG, KIEM CHING ONG • 6–8: PAINTOVER:
PIERRE-OLIVIER VINCENT

6

7

8

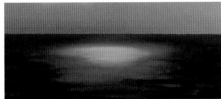

The Final Battle

The students are looking forward to their prom, but titan Nerissa has other plans that promise to make this a night to remember. While the teens prepare to party on the twin-hulled party ship, the giant mermaid engages in battle with three generations of kraken royalty, and there may be no glad tidings of great joy for them. But the tide turns in the fight. Nerissa conjures up a huge tidal wave that threatens to engulf the boat and Oceanside, but Ruby, injured but not broken, saves the day with finesse. Nerissa is vanquished, and the Trident is destroyed. It is only then that Ruby can resume her smaller size and be reunited with Connor for her promised date.

"I think the most important thing in the final battle is always driving the action through Ruby's point of view and experience as much as possible. Ruby learned a lot of cool fighting skills only in the second act, so there are things that we've done to make it clear that when Ruby shows up to save the day, we're trying to pay off those individual moments that she learned from Grandmamah when she was training with her: to swim fast, to use her body armor and ultimately her strength, and then her laser eyes—and building little moments that would highlight that she's come a long way in her training. But of course, always thinking, what does it mean for her emotionally?"
—Kirk DeMicco, Director

5

4

1, 3: Pierre-Olivier Vincent • 2: Alexandre Puvilland • 4: Timothy Lamb • 5: Simon Wells

"We don't want to have the ending turn into another superhero movie. We want to be able to check in with some of the characters right at the end to try and break it up. I want to try to avoid steady action and unending drama. We don't want to just have a ten-minute battle where somebody's going to be bored in three minutes and check out because they feel they've seen it so many times before."
—MICHELLE MENDENHALL, LEAD EDITOR

"Writing with regard to scale is one of those things in this movie that is so much fun. It works into that whole kaiju battle, where you have these big fights among these miniature buildings, and you feel that scale we're playing out. That whole fight is happening in the harbor of Oceanside, and so they're running on the seafloor, and the water is up about waist-high, and Nerissa, because she's a mermaid, is not walking—she's held up by her giant tail, which is great, and at one point, Ruby gets smashed up into a building with this Trident right at her throat, where Nerissa is trying to kill her. Nerissa uses her huge tail to send a giant tidal wave toward the prom boat, and Ruby must swim underneath that wave to pull that boat up to safety. It's a playground for a story artist to go through, and to think those things out has been so rewarding."
—GLENN HARMON, HEAD OF STORY

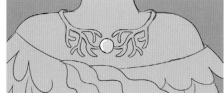

1: SURFACING RENDER ARTISTS: JEANNIE YIP CHO, BETSY ASHER HALL, RACHAEL YANG, SUSAN JONES HARRIS • 2: KATHERINE DE VRIES • 3: ALEXANDRE PUVILLAND • 4: PRODUCTION MODEL: ERIN CASWELL, EMILIE AUSTIN, SURFACING: JOHN WAKE, WOOJIN CHOI, JEREMY ENGLEMAN • 5: YURIKO OTO • 6, 7: PIERRE-OLIVIER VINCENT • 8: PRODUCTION MODEL: BEAR WILLIAMS

"In many ways I can relate to Ruby feeling like she belongs to two different worlds. I'm Franco-American, and I've moved many times and have had to figure out where I really do belong. I love the conclusion at the end, when she realizes that she belongs wherever she is, and she is who she is, and there's power in that."
—EMILIE AUSTIN, LOCATION MODELING SUPERVISOR

The Crew

CEPHALOPODS

— DREAM BIG —

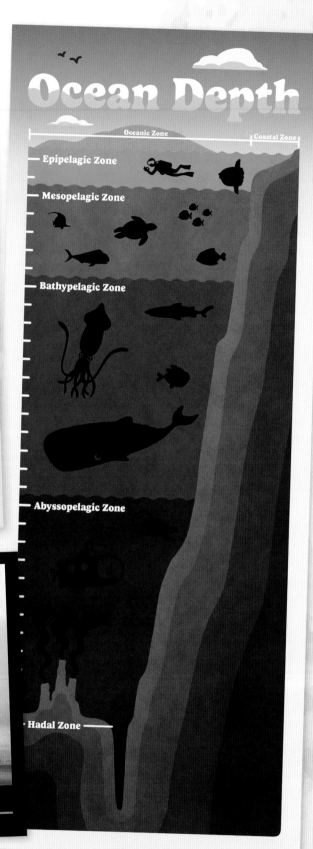

Ocean Depth

Oceanic Zone · Coastal Zone

Epipelagic Zone

Mesopelagic Zone

Bathypelagic Zone

Abyssopelagic Zone

Hadal Zone

1–3: Yuriko Oto • 4: photographer: Alex Berliner

Acknowledgments

Iain R. Morris is the creative director at Cameron + Company and has worked in the entertainment industry for over twenty-five years. He has designed numerous movie "art of" books. His first was *The Art of Star Wars: Episode II*, and he has gone on to design books for Sony Pictures Animation, 20th Century Studios, Disney, Warner Bros., and of course, DreamWorks Animation (for which he wrote *A Field Guide to the Croods: A New Age* and *The Art of The Bad Guys*), among many other companies. He lives and works in Northern California. Iain would like to thank all those at DreamWorks Animation for giving up their valuable time to help, especially Debbie Luner, Virginia Eastwood, Courtenay Guess, and Kaki Bage for being so helpful in making sure this book got done. He would also like to thank the usual suspects at work who kindly rolled their eyes at the dreadful puns herein. Take a bow, Chris Gruener, Jan Hughes, and Krista Keplinger.

DreamWorks Animation would like to thank the entire crew of *Ruby Gillman Teenage Kraken*, who worked tirelessly to create this beautiful and engaging film, along with the spectacular leadership team of Margie Cohn, Kristin Lowe, Kirk DeMicco, Kelly Cooney, Rachel Zusser, Faryn Pearl, Pierre-Oliver Vincent, Fred Stewart, Tyler Shelton, Kaki Bage, Courtney Guess, Priyaa Kalkura Thenkanidhiyur, Anna Kotyza, Mike Vollman, Courtenay Palaski, Jerry Schmitz, Michael Garcia, Debbie Luner, Virginia Eastwood, Yusef Sutton, and Lana Condor.

DreamWorks would also like to thank Chris Gruener, Iain R. Morris, Jan Hughes, Krista Keplinger, and the Cameron + Company team.

The third time's the charm, so many thanks to my parents for all their love and support. —I.R.M.

Library of Congress Cataloging-in-Publication data available.

ISBN: 978-1-4197-7020-3

10 9 8 7 6 5 4 3 2 1

Printed and bound in China

Cameron + Company

An imprint of ABRAMS
149 Kentucky Street
Suite 7, Petaluma, CA 94952

www.cameronbooks.com

PUBLISHER Chris Gruener
CREATIVE DIRECTOR Iain R. Morris
MANAGING EDITOR Jan Hughes
EDITORIAL ASSISTANT Krista Keplinger

FRONT COVER: TIMOTHY LAMB • ENDPAPERS: PIERRE-OLIVIER VINCENT • SINGLE-PAGE ENDPAPERS: FREDERIC WILLIAM STEWART • 1, 2, 5: PIERRE-OLIVIER VINCENT (AS RUBY GILLMAN) • 3: FREDERIC WILLIAM STEWART • 4, 6: VY TRINH • 7: TIMOTHY LAMB • OVERLEAF: 1: FREDERIC WILLIAM STEWART • 2: PIERRE-OLIVIER VINCENT (AS RUBY GILLMAN)

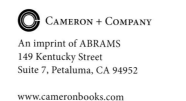

FIN